A BILL BECOMES A LAW

A BILL BECOMES A LAW

Congress Enacts Civil Rights Legislation

SECOND EDITION

DANIEL M. BERMAN
Professor of Government
The American University

THE MACMILLAN COMPANY
COLLIER-MACMILLAN LIMITED · *London*

Seventh Printing, 1971

Earlier edition, entitled *A Bill Becomes
A Law: The Civil Rights Act of 1960,*

Library of Congress catalog card number: 66-12283

The Macmillan Company
866 Third Avenue, New York, New York 10022
COLLIER-MACMILLAN CANADA, LTD., TORONTO, ONTARIO

PRINTED IN THE UNITED STATES OF AMERICA

To the Memory of My Mother

and

to My Father

PREFACE

IN THE FIRST EDITION of this book, an attempt was made to explain the functioning of Congress by describing the way in which a particular bill became law. The Civil Rights Act of 1960 was selected as the sample bill because it encountered an extraordinarily large number of the devices that are available for the purpose of passing, and defeating, legislation. An examination of the bill's history revealed that at every turn the proponents of a strong civil rights measure were blocked by procedural obstacles. The conclusion was drawn that congressional procedures possess substantive importance and may even be decisive in shaping legislation. Certainly these procedures are not merely technical devices designed to permit the Senate and House of Representatives to legislate in an orderly fashion.

The purpose of the present edition is to provide an opportunity for comparing the factors that resulted in a weak bill in 1960 with those that contributed to the shaping of a much stronger bill in 1964. To facilitate the making of comparisons, material on the 1964 act is added, wherever appropriate, to the analysis of what happened in 1960. But despite the sizable interpolations on the more recent law, the statute enacted in 1960 remains the principal subject. The reader who wants to confine his attention to that legislation should simply ignore the indented paragraphs, which are the ones devoted to 1964.

Even if the civil rights laws of 1960 and 1964 are useful samples of congressional legislation, they nevertheless are only samples. The attempt to explain the functioning of Congress by examining just these two statutes is therefore subject to an important limitation. Although the bills endured a good deal of hardship, there were some tribulations that they were spared. Thus an analysis of their progress does not throw light on every ramification of congressional procedure. In another book, *In Congress Assembled* (New York: The Macmillan Company, 1964), the author attempted to analyze more of the legislative process than can be done here. There are, in addition, several other studies of considerable value. Notable among these are the following books: *The Legislative Process in Congress,* by George B. Galloway (New York: Thomas Y. Crowell Co., 1955); *The Legislative Struggle: A Study in Social Conflict,* by Bertram M. Gross (New York: McGraw Hill Book Company, Inc., 1953); and *The American Legislative Process: Congress and the States,* by William J. Keefe and Morris S. Ogul (Englewood Cliffs, New Jersey: Prentice-Hall, Inc., 1964). A detailed description of congressional rules is contained in *The United States Congress: Organization and Procedure,* by Floyd M. Riddick (Washington: National Capitol Publishers, Inc., 1949).

The terms "conservative" and "liberal" are used many times in the present study. In other contexts, the words can mean a variety of things. Here, they are intended simply to describe opposing attitudes on the proper role of the national government. The liberal is one who (like the author) considers the use of federal power indispensable for the amelioration of economic and social inequality, while the conservative tends to think that such a recourse is usually unnecessary and always dangerous.

For such a small book, there are many large debts to acknowledge. A Congressional Fellowship of the American Political Science Association enabled me to follow the development of the Civil Rights Act of 1960 while attached to the office of a member of the House (Congressman Emanuel Celler of New York), and the staff of a Senate subcommittee (Constitutional

Rights). It also opened the door to interviews with the following members of Congress who participated in the creation of the law: Everett McKinley Dirksen of Illinois, the Republican leader in the Senate, and Charles A. Halleck of Indiana, the former Republican leader in the House; Senators Joseph S. Clark of Pennsylvania, Paul Douglas of Illinois, and Wayne Morse of Oregon, and the late Senator Estes Kefauver of Tennessee; Congressmen Richard Bolling of Missouri and John V. Lindsay of New York; former Congressman (now Secretary of the Interior) Stewart L. Udall of Arizona; and former Congressman (now Senator) Lee Metcalf of Montana. An appointment as Academic Director of the Washington Semester Program at The American University made it possible to continue observing Congress at close range during the struggle over the 1964 law, in the company of challenging and stimulating students.

Three persons read the original manuscript with such critical eyes that only inertia makes me continue to consider them friends and only tradition impels me not to blame them for errors. They are: Dr. Nathan Smith, Chairman of the Department of History and Political Science at Washington College; Dr. Alan Rosenthal, Assistant Professor of Political Science at Hunter College; and Mr. Bernard L. Sperling of Poughkeepsie, New York. My editors at Macmillan, Mr. Robert J. Patterson and Mr. Joseph Falzone, managed to combine impeccable courtesy with the necessary firmness. I express my appreciation also to Congressman (now Ambassador) James Roosevelt of California for facilitating my research. Helpful suggestions came from the late Mr. Curtis E. Johnson, Research Consultant and Assistant Staff Director of the Senate Subcommittee on Constitutional Rights; Mr. Richard C. Peet, former Minority Counsel of House Judiciary Subcommittee No. 5; and Dr. Arnold Trebach, Director of the Howard University Human Rights Program. There were important contributions from Dr. Robert E. Goostree, Professor of Law and Government at The American University; Dr. Mark Ferber, of the University of California; Dr. C. Dale Story, of Iowa State University; and

Dr. Donald Sullivan, of the United States Office of Education. The manuscript of this edition was reviewed by: Dr. Stephen Horn, Legislative Assistant to Sen. Thomas H. Kuchel; Mr. William G. Phillips, Staff Director of the Democratic Study Group; Mr. John G. Stewart, assistant to Vice President Humphrey; and Mr. Kent Watkins, Legislative Assistant to Sen. Carl Hayden and Staff Director of the Subcommittee on the Standing Rules of the Senate. One of my graduate students at The American University, Mr. J. Donald Fisher, provided me with a commendable analysis of the House Committee of the Whole; and the work of another student, Mr. Jacques DePuy, was of considerable help. The value of the secretarial services provided by Mrs. Marylee Buchly was inestimable. The assistance of Mrs. Delores A. Webber is acknowledged. I must also thank my dean, Earl H. DeLong, whose thoughtfulness manifested itself on many occasions. And I cannot neglect to mention that my preoccupation with the book subjected my wife, Aline, and my children, Stuart and Adriane, to agonies that would have been excessive for even a multi-volume work.

Gratitude of a special kind is owed to Dr. Edward McNall Burns, Professor Emeritus and former Chairman of the Department of Political Science at Rutgers University, my teacher for many years and my inspiration for many more.

D. M. B.

CONTENTS

TABLE OF DOCUMENTS

INTRODUCTION

ON MAY 6, 1960, President Eisenhower signed into law a new civil rights statute. It was a simple ceremony. Only two other persons were present: Attorney General William P. Rogers and his deputy, Lawrence E. Walsh. The statement that the President released for the occasion was prosaic and of scant news value. Even *The New York Times* did not report the event on its front page.

Not all bill-signing ceremonies are so devoid of sparkle. Occasionally, a President will crowd his office with cabinet members and influential congressmen. He will use a dozen or more pens in signing his name, so that each guest may carry away a memento. Reporters and photographers will record the drama for posterity.

But in the case of the Civil Rights Act of 1960, the absence of such flourishes was understandable, because the formal enactment of the bill was the sheerest anticlimax. Sixteen months of debating, maneuvering, and compromising had left Congress exhausted, with little capacity for enthusiasm. In its final form, the legislation provoked only the most perfunctory reactions among both friends and foes of civil rights.

IN 1964, AFTER CONGRESS HAD PASSED a far stronger civil rights law, there was considerable pomp and circumstance. Looking on as President Johnson signed the bill were the Democratic and Republican leaders of both the House and Senate, a number of cabinet officials, and some of the nation's most prominent clergymen and civil rights leaders. In addition, millions throughout the country also watched on television. During the signing ceremony, President Johnson outlined some of the preliminary steps he would take to implement the new legislation.

Despite the low key in which the signing ceremony was conducted in 1960, the bill on the President's desk was at least noteworthy in a technical sense. Since the Reconstruction, Congress had passed only one other civil rights statute, in 1957. That legislation was designed primarily to protect the Negro's right to vote—a right legally recognized since 1870. In that year, the Fifteenth Amendment had added these words to the Constitution:

> The right of citizens of the United States to vote shall not be denied or abridged by the United States or by any State on account of race, color, or previous condition of servitude.

The 1957 act attempted in several ways to breathe life into these words. It empowered the federal government to seek court injunctions against illegal interference with the franchise. It established a Civil Rights Division in the Department of Justice. And it created, as an independent agency within the executive branch, a Commission on Civil Rights, authorized to recommend remedies for unconstitutional discrimination.

Positive results of the 1957 act were not immediately apparent. When the first session of the Eighty-sixth Congress convened on January 7, 1959, the law had been on the statute books for sixteen months, but it had been used in only one case—a suit against election registrars of Terrell County, Georgia. Negro spokesmen concluded that their original skepticism about the legislation had been well founded. Their feeling that, despite appearances, the cause of civil rights had been betrayed in the Eighty-fifth Congress led them to demand that the Eighty-sixth produce something more substantial.

DECADES OF DISILLUSIONMENT

A sense of betrayal was nothing new for the Negro. The period since 1865 had been full of bitterness and frustration. At times it seemed that the only gain produced by the Civil War was the abolition of slavery ordained by the Thirteenth Amendment. In a series of decisions, the Supreme Court had eviscerated the Fourteenth Amendment, holding even that its "equal protection" clause permitted states to impose racial segregation. Moreover, despite the Fifteenth Amendment, the right to vote had remained largely a white man's privilege in the South. Only 25 per cent of all eligible Negroes were registered in 1959, as against 60 per cent of the eligible whites. In half of Mississippi's counties, not even 1 per cent of the Negroes could vote, and in those Alabama counties where Negroes outnumbered whites the proportion was only 4 per cent. Discrimination, segregation, and ostracism appeared to be the eternal lot of the Negro.

But the fact that almost one-tenth of the nation could not exercise the elementary rights of first-class citizenship was becoming increasingly awkward for the United States. World War II, allegedly waged for the sake of freedom and equality, made the embarrassment acute. In the competition with the Soviet Union that followed the war, racial discrimination became a major political liability, as a succession of newly independent nonwhite nations recoiled from the face presented to them by the United States. This prompted senators like Paul Douglas of Illinois to deplore the damage that America's reputation was suffering among the colored peoples of the world. And foreign policy was often on the mind of Attorney General Rogers when he spoke of civil rights. "We must consider the image that racial discrimination presents to a largely nonwhite world," he said. "These nations have not committed themselves to either Western ideas of democracy or to Communism. But they are watching."

The Cold War was important in another way, too. If American scientific and technological progress was to keep pace with that of the Soviet Union, efficient use of manpower and brainpower seemed essential. In this context, the denial of maximum educational opportunities to fifteen million people was illogical in the extreme.

Yet when the Supreme Court began to resuscitate the Fourteenth and Fifteenth Amendments in the forties and fifties, such considerations of foreign policy did not shield it from violent criticism. Decisions such as those that struck down "white primaries" and barred the exclusion of Negroes from juries were mere preliminaries. The climactic moment came on May 17, 1954, when Chief Justice Earl Warren announced for a unanimous court that a state violates the "equal protection" clause of the Fourteenth Amendment by maintaining all-white schools. Segregated educational facilities were "inherently unequal," for

> [t]o separate [school children] from others of similar age and qualifications solely because of their race generates a feeling of inferiority as to their status in the community that may affect their hearts and minds in a way unlikely ever to be undone.

The white South was enraged. Feeling ran so high that some even demanded the impeachment of several members of the court, particularly the Chief Justice.[1] More than one southern politician advanced his career by pledging that no school would ever be integrated in his state. As the Eighty-sixth Congress convened five years after the court's decision, token integration or no integration at all was still the rule in the South.

EFFECT OF COURT DECISION

The school decision and others that followed it, however, had a tremendous impact on the Negro. He felt at long last that the Constitution was really on his side, and that the eventual elimi-

[1] Undoubtedly one reason congressmen never took the idea seriously is that the Constitution makes the impeachment procedure exceedingly difficult. Both the House and the Senate are involved. A majority vote by the representatives suffices to "impeach" (formally charge) an official, but a two-thirds vote in the Senate is needed to convict him and remove him from office. No Supreme Court justice has ever been unseated in this way.

nation of racial barriers was inevitable. In the North, where he could vote, he was in a position to use his influence to shorten the time he would have to wait.

In some constituencies, this meant that Negroes were sent to Congress. In others, Negroes held the balance of power. Senators from states like California, New Jersey, New York, and Pennsylvania learned it was dangerous not to support civil rights, since a denunciation by Negro leaders might easily spell political death. The Negro had become a factor that could not safely be ignored.

This was especially true in presidential elections, for Negroes were concentrated in states with large blocs of electoral votes, and their strength in these states was increasing steadily as a result of migration from the South. It was understandable, therefore, that both Republicans and Democrats began to include statements on civil rights in their party platforms.

One of the many astute politicians aware of the new trend was Lyndon B. Johnson of Texas. As Senate Democratic leader in 1959, he knew that his party's chances in the presidential election of the following year might be hurt seriously if the Eighty-sixth Congress, which the Democrats controlled, failed to pass civil rights legislation. His concern for the party was fortified by another consideration. The major stumbling block to his own pursuit of the presidential nomination in 1960 was his identification with the South. A personal record on civil rights that could not be branded "typically southern" would be highly advantageous.

INTERESTINGLY ENOUGH, the same thought was in Johnson's mind when he succeeded to the presidency upon the death of John F. Kennedy in November 1963. With the next presidential election only a year away, the new Chief Executive was acutely aware of the suspicion with which he was regarded by civil rights supporters, whose votes had been necessary for Mr. Kennedy to win the election of 1960. He felt, however, that if he steered a strong civil rights bill through Congress, he might finally be looked upon as a nationally minded statesman rather than a provincial southern politician.

As the leader of his party in the Senate in 1959, Johnson was convinced that the Eighty-sixth Congress should pass a civil rights bill. In his view, the proper time for action was during the first session. He reasoned that the party's presidential chances could be seriously weakened if the Democrats had to reveal their bitter sectional differences in 1960, only a few months before the election.

Thus, as Congress assembled, it was generally assumed that a civil rights bill of some kind would be approved. Only one question remained: would it materially aid the cause of the Negro, or would it be merely a token measure designed to do little else than portray its sponsors as champions of civil rights?

Suggestions for Legislation

THE DEMOCRATS had more than comfortable majorities in both houses of the Eighty-sixth Congress, just as they were to have in 1963, when the question of civil rights would next be raised. Yet they were in no position to enact important legislation unaided. This was so because many of their southern members rarely voted with the rest of the party on economic and social legislation. Certainly on the issue of civil rights, the northern Democrats would need Republican support if a majority was to be mustered.

In deciding whether to render such support, Republicans would of course look to President Eisenhower for guidance. The President's first formal opportunity to advise the new Congress came with his State of the Union address in January. Mr. Eisenhower, however, did not make use of the occasion to plead the cause of Negro equality. Although he announced that civil rights proposals would soon be sent to Congress, he limited himself for the moment to the comment that significant progress toward equality of opportunity had already been registered. "That progress must continue," he said.

NOTHING MORE SUBSTANTIAL was contained in the State of the Union address delivered by President Kennedy four years later. The Democratic President demonstrated little more enthusiasm for civil rights legislation than had his Republican predecessor. The only aspect of civil rights on which he even touched was voting. And on this subject he merely expressed the feeling that the franchise "must not be denied to any citizens on grounds of their race or their color" and that "all those who are willing to vote should always be permitted."

Mr. Eisenhower had at least promised a special message on civil rights, and one month after his State of the Union address he submitted it. The message recommended enactment of a seven-point civil rights program. Nothing the program contained, however, excited as much comment as one omission. The President had failed to repeat his 1957 request that Congress authorize the Attorney General to bring civil court actions for the protection of individual rights.

Proponents of a strong bill had fought bitterly for that legislation in 1957. Without doubt, Part III (as it was labeled) had been the heart of the President's earlier program. The federal government would be given the power, under its provisions, to *prevent* interference with civil rights instead of being able only to *punish* such interference after the event. At the same time, Part III would relieve the Negro of the need to institute his own complaints in civil rights cases: the Attorney General, acting on his own initiative, could ask in federal court for an injunction prohibiting any threatened violation, and disregard of such an order could be punished as contempt of court. But despite administration backing for this legislation, Congress had refused to enact it in 1957. Only in voting cases did it empower the Attorney General to seek injunctive relief. Mr. Eisenhower's decision not to renew his sponsorship of Part III in 1959 made it unlikely that more would be done now.

PRESIDENTIAL PROPOSALS

Three of the points that Mr. Eisenhower did recommend in 1959 concerned schools. The President asked Congress to make it a crime for one to interfere, by the threat or actual use of force, with a school desegregation order of a federal court. He also wanted authorization for the government to provide free education for children of military personnel if the public schools they had been attending were closed to avoid integration. And he asked Congress to accept formally the principle that the Constitution as interpreted by the Supreme Court is the highest law of the land. Accordingly, he said, state and local governments should be reminded of their obligation to move toward school desegregation, and the federal government should agree to defray part of the cost of liquidating the segregated schools.

Only one item on Mr. Eisenhower's list dealt with voting, which had been the principal subject of the 1957 law. The recommendation he made was prompted by the fact that some southern officials, in order to hamper investigations by the Department of Justice and the Civil Rights Commission, had been destroying or impounding voting and registration records. The President proposed that Congress require states to preserve such records for three years when they pertained to federal elections.

There were requests in the presidential message for several other actions: a two-year extension of the Civil Rights Commission, which would otherwise expire later in 1959; the creation of a permanent commission to combat job discrimination in companies with government contracts; and the establishment of penalties for interstate flight to avoid prosecution for bombing a church or school.

PRESIDENT KENNEDY changed his mind and sent a civil rights message to Congress, too, after delivering his State of the Union address. The specific recommendations he made, however, were as modest as those of Mr. Eisenhower. Apart from asking Congress to prolong the life of the Civil Rights Commission, he only suggested "technical and financial assistance to aid school districts in the process of desegregation," and legislation that would protect the right to vote. And even this minimal program was not on the White House list of high-priority legislation. Administration spokesmen, in fact, let it be known in Congress that Mr. Kennedy wanted to avoid a fight over civil rights, for that might very well complicate the campaign for "more pressing" legislation, such as the tax-reduction bill which the President was promoting.

AVAILABLE ALTERNATIVES

While congressmen who belong to the party of the President tend to look to the White House for guidance on legislative questions, members of the party out of power generally allow their congressional leadership to set their course. Thus in 1959 it was to be expected that on a subject like civil rights the Democrats would go along with the Senate Majority Leader, Lyndon Johnson, and the Speaker of the House, Sam Rayburn. Although Rayburn did not express himself on the subject until much later,[2] his fellow Texan had introduced a civil rights bill of his own even before the President had acted. With regard to the crucial Part III, Johnson went no further than Mr. Eisenhower: he, too, omitted it from his bill. In several other respects, his measure was not even as strong as the one sponsored by the President. For one thing, it would prolong the life of the Civil Rights Commission for only fifteen months instead of two years. And, more important, it would deal obliquely rather than frontally with the school problem.

The indirect approach that Johnson favored regarding schools (as well as other aspects of the race issue) emphasized the progress that might be made through conciliation. To help communities divided by racial conflict, the majority leader would set up a Federal Community Relations Service, which would offer its assistance as a mediator between whites and

---

2 Rayburn, in fact, chose to remain somewhat in the background during the entire civil rights battle. One reason was that he wanted his protégé, Senator Johnson, to command the center of the stage and thus improve his chances of obtaining the 1960 Democratic presidential nomination. But even when this kind of factor is absent, a Speaker exercises most of his often decisive power quietly. He is especially effective in his role as leader of the majority party in the House, which elects him to office. The speakership is not quite as important as it was before 1911, when the House rebelled against the dictatorial Joe Cannon; it is still sufficiently influential, however, so that no one who holds it is tempted to seek any other position, except perhaps the presidency.

Negroes. Although his bill contained two other provisions,[3] the senator attached the greatest importance to his conciliation proposal because it employed what he called "the tools of peaceful persuasion." His enthusiasm, however, was by no means universally shared. Representatives of fifty organizations, united as the Leadership Conference on Civil Rights, characterized the mediation plan as "definitely a step backward" and "not even a compromise." One of their spokesmen went so far as to declare that it would be better to have no bill at all. Johnson assailed these critics for insisting that "everything should be done at once—or nothing." They wanted only to make an impression, he charged; his aim was to achieve results.

A passionate denunciation of the Majority Leader came from Senator Douglas of Illinois. He attacked Johnson for not dealing directly with the problem of school desegregation. To be neutral on this question, he said, was not a compromise, but a "surrender of the leadership which the people have a right to expect from Congress." With a number of liberal senators in agreement with Douglas that the efforts of Johnson, like those of the President, had fallen short of the mark, sixteen of them joined in bipartisan sponsorship of an alternative draft. Its most important feature was Part III, missing in both of the rival bills. Another provision would express approval of Supreme Court decisions outlawing a wide variety of Jim Crow practices.

Three major proposals for civil rights legislation were now before Congress.

Committee Action in the House

THE FIRST HEARINGS on the competing bills were conducted in the House, which (like the Senate) puts civil rights within the

---

[3] One would permit the Attorney General to subpoena documents that he needed for the preparation of voting rights cases. The other would make it a federal crime to transport explosives intended for illegal purposes from one state to another.

jurisdiction of its Judiciary Committee. Along with many other overburdened committees, Judiciary follows the practice of authorizing subcommittees to screen legislation before the full committee acts. Though each Judiciary subcommittee specializes in a particular type of legislation (such as patents, immigration, and antitrust), this specialization is not absolute.[4] At any time, the committee chairman is free to ignore it. If, for example, he wants to deal personally with a certain group of bills, he may very well decide that they should be referred to the subcommittee on which he himself sits, irrespective of its customary function. That was precisely what happened in the case of the civil rights bills. Since the Judiciary Committee's chairman, as well as its ranking (senior) Republican, sat on Subcommittee No. 5, and since both were keenly interested in the subject of civil rights, it was to that subcommittee that the bills were assigned.

Chairman of the subcommittee was Congressman Emanuel Celler, who was also head of the parent Judiciary Committee. Celler's district in Brooklyn contained a heavy representation of ethnic, racial, and religious minorities. In such a constituency, his reputation as an influential friend of civil rights and a champion of liberalism virtually assured perpetual reelection. He had represented the district for 36 years; only two of his fellow Democrats had been in Congress longer. His victory in the election of 1958, when he won 81.4 per cent of the votes cast, was typical.

While making a reputation as a fighter for civil rights, Celler, like many liberals in Congress, continued to bask in the friendship of his southern colleagues. In common with other Democrats who possessed seniority and held positions of power, he had a close relationship with the party leadership. He enjoyed an unusually high degree of acceptance because, although he spoke for liberal principles, he conscientiously avoided strain-

---

[4] The Judiciary Committee's counterpart in the Senate does follow the principle of unqualified specialization. Its subcommittees limit themselves to definite subjects like constitutional amendments, internal security, immigration and naturalization, and constitutional rights.

ing party unity. He was first, last, and always an organization man.

In his public pronouncements, however, Celler could be counted on to advocate the strongest type of civil rights legislation, and it was only natural that his bill—like the one Douglas was sponsoring in the Senate—contained the significant provisions of Part III. Like their chairman, most members of the subcommittee found it easy to support civil rights. In contrast to the full committee, one-third of whose members were from the South, the subcommittee was completely northern in composition, and thus provided a convenient sounding board for witnesses advocating far-reaching civil rights measures.

SUBCOMMITTEE HEARINGS

Almost all those who testified before the subcommittee represented liberal organizations such as labor unions, the American Veterans' Committee, the B'nai B'rith Anti-Defamation League, and the National Association for the Advancement of Colored People. The witnesses were generally well received. Seldom during the public hearings did they have to cope with probing questions. One exception was Roy Wilkins, executive secretary of the NAACP, who was challenged repeatedly by Congressman William E. Miller of New York, a vigorously partisan Republican (later to become national committee chairman and still later the vice-presidential running mate of Barry M. Goldwater). Miller told Wilkins, who had argued for the approval of Part III, that this provision was doomed because of the opposition of Senator Johnson, the Democratic leader. Civil rights advocates, he said, should abandon utopian goals and work for the Republican Administration's bill, which he insisted was the strongest measure with a chance of passage.

The most important witness for the administration was Attorney General Rogers. His testimony made it clear that the administration would not change its position on Part III. Broadening the use of the injunction procedure, he said, could prove unwise, for the "image of the federal government attempting to dominate the states" might provoke people unnecessarily and "harden their resistance to the point where it makes any reasonable solution difficult."

If witnesses speaking for civil rights [5] received gentle treatment, southerners felt outnumbered. Congressman James C. Davis of Georgia charged bluntly: "The subcommittee is stacked." Another representative who testified was equally bitter in his comment. Congressman L. Mendel Rivers of South Carolina complained that the South could expect little sympathy for its position. "We recognize," he said, "that for all intents and purposes your report is made and your decision is made so far as we are concerned. . . . We have been 'hanged, drawn, and quartered,' as Shakespeare would say, in absentia."

Although subcommittee members refrained from questioning Rivers about Shakespeare, they made few other concessions to southern sensibilities. Taking care always to be elaborately polite, they did not even try to conceal the fact that they were intent on approving some sort of civil rights bill from the variety under consideration.

THE SAME SUBCOMMITTEE dealt with civil rights in 1963. During the early stages of its hearings, an air of complete unreality prevailed, for there could be no action without firm support from the Kennedy Administration, and that support was not forthcoming. But developments were taking place that would change this, and in a most dramatic way. For while the subcommittee hearings were in progress, the South erupted in a series of racial incidents which suddenly pushed the civil rights issue to the center of the stage and compelled the Administration to reexamine its do-nothing policy.

What was happening in Birmingham, Alabama was particularly difficult to ignore. With the Negro community demonstrating for an end to racial discrimina-

---

[5] The pro-civil rights witnesses also included Arthur S. Flemming, Secretary of Health, Education, and Welfare, and two Negro members of the House.

tion, local officials tried to cope with a complex social situation in simple police terms. They arrested 700 school children who had participated in a protest march, and made use of fire hoses and police dogs against adults. When, on top of all this, bombs were thrown at the home of a brother of Dr. Martin Luther King, chaos seemed imminent.

Although hundreds of state troopers were dispatched to Birmingham, the situation continued to deteriorate, and President Kennedy said he was considering whether or not federal military forces specially trained in riot control should be sent in. The Chief Executive demonstrated his resoluteness by actually moving troops to military bases near Birmingham, and after this the situation abated somewhat.

But Alabama's troubles were far from over. One month after the Birmingham crisis, the President was compelled to place the Alabama National Guard under federal control in order to prevent Governor George C. Wallace from frustrating a court order admitting two Negro students to the University of Alabama.

The events in Alabama, as well as pressure from a number of Republicans for legislative action, persuaded Mr. Kennedy to make the forceful commitment to civil rights legislation he had so assiduously avoided in the past. Just a few hours after the two students had been registered at the University of Alabama, he spoke on radio and television to make an appeal both to conscience and to enlightened self-interest. The appeal to conscience was eloquent:

> . . . The Negro baby born in America today . . . has about one-half as much chance of completing high school as a white baby born in the same place on the same day . . ., twice as much chance of becoming unemployed . . ., a life expectancy which is seven years shorter, and the prospects of earning only half as much.

The appeal to enlightened self-interest was frank:

> The events in Birmingham and elsewhere have so increased the cries for equality that no city or state or legislative body can prudently choose to ignore them. The fires of frustration and discord are burning in every city, North and South, where legal remedies are not at hand. Redress is sought in the streets in demonstrations, parades, and protests which create tensions and threaten violence and threaten lives.

The President announced that he had decided to ask Congress for broad civil rights legislation providing legal remedies for discrimination in education, voting, and public accommodations.

One week later, Mr. Kennedy spelled out exactly what he wanted. In a special message to Congress, he recommended legislation that went far beyond what he had asked for earlier in the year. Equal access to public accommodations should be guaranteed, he now said, and the government should be given legal weapons to protect this right. The Attorney General should also be empowered, under certain circumstances, to file legal suits himself to desegregate public schools instead of having to wait for private parties to institute litigation. And the administrator of every federal program should be permitted to withhold financial assistance from any state activity in which racial discrimination was being practiced.

It was clear to everyone that the Administration was really serious this time. When House Judiciary Subcommittee No. 5 resumed its civil rights hearings, it tackled its work with a zealousness and determination that had been entirely absent in the earlier phase.

REVOLT OF THE MASSES

During the subcommittee's hearings in 1959, thirty-nine bills were on the agenda. Although each bore a different number, there was much overlapping and duplication. This is a common phenomenon in the House, which does not follow the Senate's practice of permitting several members to co-sponsor a single bill. Each congressman who wants his name associated with a measure must introduce it on his own, even though it may be identical with those sponsored by others. Thus the large number of bills nominally before the subcommittee was somewhat misleading. Moreover, it is usual for a committee to consider seriously only legislation that has been introduced by a senior congressman (particularly if he is the committee's own chairman or its ranking minority member). Accordingly, the testimony in Subcommittee No. 5 tended to center around only two bills: H.R. 3147,[6] introduced by Chairman Celler, and H.R. 4457, offered by Congressman William M. McCulloch of Ohio, the senior Republican on the Judiciary Committee. Of these two bills, Celler's alone contained the Part III provision (empowering the Attorney General to seek federal court injunctions against those who might interfere with civil rights); McCulloch's was confined to the seven-point program that Mr. Eisenhower had recommended.

IN 1963, THE SUBCOMMITTEE was inundated with 158 separate bills, but witnesses usually addressed themselves to the Administration version, introduced in the House

---

[6] The "H.R." designation is used for bills originating in the House of Representatives, while "S." identifies Senate bills. The initials are applied to both "public bills" (legislation dealing with subjects of general significance like taxes, labor relations, or civil rights) and "private bills" (those providing relief for single individuals).

Other types of legislative measures have identifying initials as well:

1. "H.J. Res." is a "joint resolution" originating in the House; "S.J. Res.," one initiated by the Senate. Joint resolutions have the same force as public bills and, like them, are submitted to the President for his signature. They are usually simple, one-purpose enactments, such as extensions of statutes due to expire.

2. "H. Con. Res." and "S. Con. Res." signify "concurrent resolutions." These involve matters that directly affect only Congress, not the public (e.g., a resolution to schedule a joint session, or to adjourn at a particular time). Such resolutions are not submitted to the President.

3. "H. Res." and "S. Res." identify "simple resolutions," in which a single chamber takes an action within its own scope (e.g., the House creates a new committee, or the Senate expresses its opinion on a foreign policy issue).

CIVIL RIGHTS

HEARINGS

BEFORE

SUBCOMMITTEE NO. 5

OF THE

COMMITTEE ON THE JUDICIARY
HOUSE OF REPRESENTATIVES

EIGHTY-SIXTH CONGRESS

FIRST SESSION

ON

H.R. 300, 351, 352, 353, 400, 430, 461, 617, 618, 619, 759, 913, 914, 1902, 2346, 2479, 2538, 2786, 3090, 3147, 3148, 3212, 3559, 4169, 4261, 4338, 4339, 4342, 4348, 4457, 5008, 5170, 5189, 5217, 5218, 5276, 5323, 6934, 6935

MISCELLANEOUS BILLS REGARDING THE CIVIL RIGHTS OF PERSONS WITHIN THE JURISDICTION OF THE UNITED STATES

MARCH 4, 5, 11, 12, 13, 18, 19; APRIL 14, 15, 16, 17, 22, 23, 24, 29, 30; MAY 1, 1959

Serial No. 5

Printed for the use of the Committee on the Judiciary

UNITED STATES
GOVERNMENT PRINTING OFFICE
56106 O WASHINGTON : 1959

Title page of House Judiciary Subcommittee hearings. List of 39 bills and dates of hearings in March, April, May, 1959.

by Chairman Celler. Testimony in favor of that bill came from an imposing group of Cabinet officers: Attorney General Robert F. Kennedy; W. Willard Wirtz, Secretary of Labor; and Anthony J. Celebrezze, Secretary of Health, Education, and Welfare.

The hearings conducted by the House Judiciary Subcommittee in 1959 lasted for seventeen days, extending over a period of three months. After they had been concluded, the subcommittee went into executive session. The eventual draft that it approved was ostensibly a compromise between the Celler and McCulloch bills. Part III, the major provision of the Celler bill, was retained, but in other respects the new measure duplicated the Eisenhower-McCulloch proposals. Technically, however, the items sponsored by the Republicans were considered merely amendments to H.R. 3147, the Celler bill.

Advocates of strong legislation were generally content with the revision that the subcommittee had approved. But there was no inclination to celebrate. The full committee could easily undo what the subcommittee had accomplished.

CELLER AND MC CULLOCH were the central figures in the subcommittee in 1963 as they had been in 1959, but neither of the two was prepared for what would happen. Partly because of the outrages that were continuing in the South, the subcommittee members surprised everyone by strengthening the Administration bill instead of diluting it, as had been forecast on all sides. For instance, a prohibition against job discrimination—endorsed earlier by the Committee on Education and Labor—was added to the Administration bill, although President Kennedy had decided against a fair employment section. But that was not all. The subcommittee also revived the Part III provision, allowing the Attorney General to seek an injunction in federal court against any civil rights violation. Moreover, it recommended that voting be protected in state as well as federal elections, and that the Civil Rights Commission be made a permanent agency instead of having its life extended for only a few years.

Those who voted in favor of the broad subcommittee bill made up a heterogeneous group. Included in that group were a number of liberal Democrats. These members, dedicated for many years to the cause of Negro equality, had suddenly found themselves under heavy pressure from civil rights organizations, which made the point that the time had never been more favorable for a frontal legislative assault on racial discrimination. In the group there were also some northern Republicans, who were firmly resolved that the Democrats should not be permitted to claim the credit for whatever law eventually emerged. And lastly a handful of anti-civil rights southern Democrats contributed their votes, in the belief that strengthening the Administration bill was the best way to assure that the bill would never pass. It was this peculiar coalition which approved the legislation that was sent to the parent Judiciary Committee.

ACTION BY JUDICIARY COMMITTEE

On civil rights, the Judiciary Committee was more conservative than either Subcommittee No. 5 or the House as a whole, largely because it contained a disproportionate number of southerners. Therefore, as might have been anticipated, it decided in 1959 to approve a measure vastly different from the one that had been recommended by the subcommittee. Four critical provisions were dropped: the vital Part III authorization; the program of financial assistance for communities making progress toward school desegregation; the endorsement of the Supreme Court's school decision; and the plan to give statutory authority to the already existing presidential commission against job discrimination by government contractors.[7]

What remained was organized into six "titles." In essence, they provided for the following:

Title I. A fine of as much as $1,000 and imprisonment up to sixty days for interference with a school desegregation order of a federal court.

Title II. A fine of $5,000 and a jail term of five years for fleeing across state lines after bombing any building.

Title III. Preservation for two years of records pertaining to the election of federal officials, and their availability to the Department of Justice.

Title IV. A two-year extension of the Civil Rights Commission, with a new authorization to take sworn testimony.

Title V. Educational opportunities furnished by the federal government for children of military personnel in areas where regular schools had been closed to prevent desegregation.

Title VI. Separability of the various titles. (This meant that if the Supreme Court invalidated any portion of the act, the other provisions would still remain in force.)

When a committee makes drastic alterations in legislation that it has been dealing with, it often frames a completely new bill. Such a "clean bill" is then introduced by a member of the committee and given a new number. It was Celler who introduced the new six-point measure, which was accorded the designation H.R. 8601.

CHAIRMAN CELLER ANTICIPATED that the full committee would act in 1963 as it had done in 1959 and whittle down the bill reported out by the subcommittee. That would actually be all to the good, he reasoned, for the subcommittee bill had some features that might alienate the moderates in the House, and support from them would be indispensable on the floor. Attorney General Kennedy agreed with Celler. When he appeared

7 The last of the omissions was prompted at least partly by the fact that the Democrats did not want to give added prestige to a body headed by Vice President Richard M. Nixon.

before the committee in executive session, he criticized the subcommittee draft in almost every detail. "What I want is a bill," he emphasized. The NAACP wanted a bill, too, but it was more optimistic than the Attorney General about what Congress would be willing to accept, and its analysis was commanding more and more support in the committee. There was, in fact, a real possibility that the full committee would adopt the subcommittee bill.

In an effort to resolve the differences between the Administration and the proponents of the subcommittee draft, intensive bipartisan negotiations were initiated. Participating in the talks together with Celler and McCulloch were the top Democrats in the House, Speaker John W. McCormack and Majority Leader Carl Albert, and the principal Republican leaders. Before long, President Kennedy decided to enter into the dispute and summoned to the White House the leaders, the rank-and-file committee members, and Vice President Johnson. Such a bipartisan meeting with the President on a domestic issue was extremely unusual and emphasized the gravity of the situation.

The White House meeting soon made it clear to Mr. Kennedy that the supporters of the subcommittee bill would not permit themselves to be dissuaded. Because he was a realist, the President reluctantly agreed under those circumstances to accept a compromise measure that had much in common with the subcommittee bill, and that measure was soon approved by the full Judiciary Committee. The tenacity of the all-out civil rights advocates on the committee had served the cause of the Negro well.

Without any doubt, the compromise bill was far stronger than the legislation originally proposed by the Administration. For example, it contained a section on discrimination in employment, a subject from which the Administration had shied away completely. In addition, a modified version of Part III was included: the Attorney General would be allowed to lodge suits on his own to desegregate public facilities, and he would also be able to intervene in suits brought by others alleging that they had been deprived of equal protection of the laws. Moreover, the provision for dealing with racial discrimination in the use of federal funds had acquired new teeth. Mr. Kennedy had originally asked only for discretionary authority to prevent discrimination in programs run with the aid of federal funds; the compromise went considerably further and imposed a mandatory obligation on executive agencies to prevent any federally financed project from withholding benefits because of race. And while the Administration had requested only a four-year extension of the Civil Rights Commission, the substitute measure provided for the Commission to become a permanent agency.

Although some said that the compromise bill did not go quite as far as the subcommittee bill, it could not be disputed that civil rights legislation had emerged from the Judiciary Committee in better form than it had entered. At least as important, the circumstances under which the new bill was drawn up made it unlikely that the compromise would be weakened on the House floor —and perhaps not in the Senate, either—for the bipartisan group that had produced it was pledged to stand united against all but the most minor changes. Moderates in the House felt that they had been "sold down the river" in 1957 and 1960, when they had ignored the political risks and worked to develop a reasonably strong bill, only to have the Senate amputate its key provisions. This, they were resolved, would not be allowed to happen again.

Certainly Congressman McCulloch, without whom the compromise bill could never have been devised, was not ready to retreat. A matter of pride was involved. McCulloch, who had almost no Negro constituents, represented an Ohio district that cared very little about civil rights. Yet he had labored long and hard for the bill. The legislation was thus "a product of his undiluted principle," as a writer in the *New Republic* put it, and it was understandable that he would refuse to settle for anything less.

Fully cognizant of how important it would be to retain such bipartisan backing for the bill, President Kennedy expressed warm appreciation to McCulloch and also to Congressman Charles A. Halleck, the Minority Leader. And Robert Kennedy added of the two Republicans: "In my judgment, if it had not been for their support and effort, the possibility of civil rights legislation in Congress would have been remote."

FILING OF REPORT

Every major item of legislation that comes to the floor of the House is buttressed by a printed committee report. This document serves as a detailed explanation of the bill and as a means of rallying support. The Judiciary Committee in 1959 submitted H.R. 8601 to the House with a report defending it—not from liberals who might consider that it was not strong enough, but from southerners to whom it appeared a threat even in its weakened form.

The committee denied that the legislation was aimed at any particular section of the country or segment of the population. "Its scope is national and its applicability general," the report said. The bill would merely provide "adequate tools for the protection of rights and privileges guaranteed by the Constitution and the laws of the United States, particularly with regard to the right to vote."

Several sets of minority views accompanied the committee report. Two Republicans from the East joined in labeling the bill "a bare minimum," while approving what it did contain. They called for restoration of the parts that had been eliminated. Another Republican criticized the committee for broadening the antibombing provision to cover cases that were not properly the concern of the federal government.[8]

Ten southerners on the committee subscribed to minority views challenging the very basis of the legislation. Although they applauded the committee for having refined and improved the subcommittee draft, their disagreement with the bill was too deep-seated to be overcome by any amendments. "This legislation," they wrote, "is fundamentally wrong and can never be made right. [It] is bad in principle, and any mitigation of the evil still leaves the quintessence of evil." The southern dissenters provided a bill of particulars: the section on obstruction of court orders interfered with freedom of speech; the general antibombing provision was out of place in a civil rights bill; Congress lacked constitutional authority to insist that states retain election records; the Civil Rights Commission, which had created "ill feelings on the part of many of our people," did not deserve an extension; and the arrangement for emergency schooling was a "backdoor approach" to federal control of education.

Chairman Celler did not file additional views. Although he criticized the attenuated bill as woefully inadequate, he insisted that he could get the committee to accept nothing stronger. Actually, he said, a great victory had been won. He argued that the bill contained several valuable elements even without Part III. And it had importance beyond its specific provisions, he added. It would bring the civil rights issue to the floor and thus open the way for strengthening amendments, including Part III.

A VOLUMINOUS SET of reports accompanied the civil rights bill to the House floor in 1963. The Judiciary Committee submitted a majority report and also a number of other statements containing the views of

[8] He believed that the destruction of schools and places of worship presented important national problems, since racial and religious intolerance were of general concern; other destructive actions, on the other hand, were local offenses, best handled by state and municipal authorities.

members who either opposed the bill or wished to express their concurrence in their own way. Altogether, there were seven statements filed.

Role of House Rules Committee

ALTHOUGH H.R. 8601—the 1959 bill—had been approved by the Judiciary Committee, there was still no assurance that it would ever reach the floor of the House. Before that could happen, it would have to be given clearance by the Rules Committee.

When a bill is reported out by a committee, it is placed on one of the three regular House "calendars," depending on the nature of the material with which it deals. If it is not an item of general legislation, it is listed on the Private Calendar. Public bills that involve the raising or spending of money go on the Union Calendar, while those not concerned with financial matters are put on the House Calendar.

On each calendar, bills are listed in chronological order. This arrangement, however, does not determine when they will reach the floor (except for bills on the Private Calendar). Nor does a listing even assure that a bill will be debated or voted upon at all. When legislation is not likely to excite controversy, there is a simple and efficient procedure for bringing it before the House.[9] But a bill that cannot anticipate nearly unanimous approval must travel a hard road.

---

[9] A motion by any member suffices to include such legislation on the special Consent Calendar. Twice a month, the bills on this calendar are placed before the House. When a bill is reached, it is considered to have been passed if no objection is heard. A single protest means that action is postponed until the next call of the calendar. At that time, three objections are required to prevent passage. If the bill is once again blocked, it is dropped from the Consent Calendar for the rest of the congressional session. It remains, however, on one of the regular calendars.

A procedure has been established to prevent legislation opposed by either the majority or minority leadership from slipping through on the Consent Calendar. Each leader designates three members of his party as "objectors," and these are expected to be present each day the Consent Calendar is called.

The normal method for bringing a controversial bill to the floor—the one that was used for H.R. 8601—is to ask the Rules Committee to recommend a "rule" under which it may be considered. Such a rule specifies, among other things, the amount of time to be allowed for debate and whether amendments may be added on the floor. Few bills reach the stage of House consideration without the consent of the Rules Committee. Since committees in every Congress report out far more bills than there is time to debate, someone has to decide which ones deserve to be cleared for the floor, in what order they should be brought up, and how much time can be devoted to each. The Rules Committee performs this task of scheduling legislation.

For many years, the committee operated as an instrument of the majority party in discharging this responsibility. It seemed reasonable that the party to which the voters had given control of the House should be master of the legislative program. The Rules Committee, therefore, was exempted from the normal practice that committee seats be apportioned to Democrats and Republicans on the basis of the strength each party possesses in the House as a whole. Instead, the majority party in the House—regardless of how narrow its margin of control might be—would fill eight of the twelve seats on the Rules Committee.

CONSERVATIVE COALITION

An entirely new factor, however, was introduced during the midthirties. In revolt against the New Deal, southern Democrats on the Rules Committee began to vote with their Republican colleagues. The conservative alliance thus forged made the committee a graveyard for liberal legislation, even when the Democrats dominated the House.

In the Eighty-sixth Congress, this bipartisan barricade against civil rights and social welfare was manned by six congressmen. Their votes were enough to block action, since seven of the twelve committee members had to concur for a bill to be sent to the House.

Each of the four Republicans on the committee was a faithful member of the conservative coalition. The GOP leadership never placed any liberals on the Rules Committee. Like the leaders themselves, those who were selected always possessed impeccably conservative credentials.

Yet the Republicans on the committee would have remained only an impotent minority if the Democrats had chosen to give seven of their eight seats to liberals. The majority party, however, would not ignore its southern members. Thus, in the Eighty-sixth Congress, two ultraconservative southerners—Howard W. Smith of Virginia and William Colmer of Mississippi—were among the Democrats on the Rules Committee. Smith, as a matter of fact, was chairman.

The Virginian did not hesitate to use his chairmanship to advance conservative aims. As he once put it, his constituents had not sent him to Washington "to be a traffic cop." He would not be content with the relatively insignificant job of keeping the legislative highways open.[10] One of his favorite tactics to bar liberal legislation from the floor was to disappear from the capital and thus prevent the committee from even meeting. That was precisely what he had done during one phase of the civil rights struggle in 1957. When Speaker Rayburn heard that Smith had allegedly gone to Virginia to inspect a barn that had burned on his farm, he reportedly commented: "I knew Howard Smith would do most anything to block a civil rights bill, but I never suspected he would resort to arson."

House members who did not want to stand up and be counted on sensitive political issues were grateful to the Rules Committee for the role it was playing. Congressmen with liberal constituencies but conservative personal philosophies, for example, could curry favor with voters by speaking pas-

---

10 Few serious students think that the "traffic cop" analogy is apt. It assumes that a Rules Committee could—or should—operate on the premise that all bills are to be treated equally, with each given as clear a road as the volume of traffic will permit. Bertram M. Gross, in *The Legislative Struggle: A Study in Social Conflict* (New York: McGraw Hill, 1953, p. 90), objects that "legislative traffic in Congress cannot be compared to that of automobiles on a highway, where the right-of-way is generally given without examination of a vehicle's destination or cargo." If Gross is correct, it is frivolous to question the committee's need for discretionary power; the real issue is whether the committee, in view of its great power, should not be responsible to the leadership of the majority party.

sionately for a liberal bill, while remaining serene in the knowledge that the Rules Committee would never permit the bill to come to the floor. Smith once said:

> Some folks might be surprised to know the number of people from both sides of the aisle, who have, under deep stress about bills, come to me and said: "Judge, we wish you'd take another vacation. We'll get up a pot and pay for it." This year, everybody I think that came to see me wanted to help paint my barn or something like that. . . .[11]

Of all liberal legislation, the kind that Smith liked least concerned civil rights. It was not unexpected, therefore, that when Celler formally petitioned his committee to grant a rule for H.R. 8601, a stone wall was promptly erected. It soon became apparent that the chairman did not even intend that the committee should meet to discuss the matter. Experience had taught Celler and his followers that it would be a waste of time to apply delicate pressures to this committee. Conscious of this fact, they initiated a procedure that was anything but subtle. They filed with the House a "discharge petition."

TO SIGN OR NOT TO SIGN

If successful, a discharge petition thwarts a committee's efforts to prevent the House from considering a bill. Any House member may present a motion that a given committee be "discharged" of further responsibility for a particular measure. His

---

[11] Ernest S. Griffith, former director of the Legislative Reference Service of the Library of Congress, defends the theory that some measures should be kept from the floor, where constituency pressures might force their enactment. He writes:

> In a democratic, representative government in this day and age, it seems to be a practical necessity that ways and means be found whereby an elected representative, desirous of serving the broader public interest, can avoid taking positions publicly on issues strongly felt by minorities, if the positions thus urged are regarded by the representative as not in line with general welfare.

Dr. Griffith believes that when the Rules Committee blockades a bill, it is frequently doing precisely what a majority of the House favor but cannot afford to admit. If the committee has "misjudged the temper of the House," he notes, that majority need only sign a discharge petition. *Congress: Its Contemporary Role* (New York: New York University Press, 1961), 27.

petition remains on the Speaker's desk, where congressmen in favor of wresting the bill from committee may sign it. If more than half of all the representatives feel strongly enough to do so and if this majority retains its strength for a confirmatory vote on the floor, the bill is dislodged from committee and sent to the whole House for debate and decision.

Although this procedure does not appear to be especially complicated, few bills are freed from committee through its use. Of those that do come to the floor as a result of discharge petitions, virtually none can overcome all the other legislative obstacles and attain final congressional enactment. Actually, on only two occasions in the history of Congress have bills become law after successful discharge petitions in the House.[12]

A petition hardly ever gets the requisite number of signatures, because highly practical considerations stand in the way. The average congressman tends to conform. He recognizes the danger of displeasing committee chairmen, for they often can decide the fate of legislation affecting his own political future (such as private bills requested by important constituents). He knows also that he is setting a precedent he may regret, for some day one of *his* committees may be threatened by a discharge petition against a bill that *he* wants to keep from the floor.

Prejudice against signing is so great that a congressman who resists it and touches pen to paper may feel like a veritable iconoclast. If such a feeling does not overwhelm him spontaneously, his senior colleagues are quick to point out that he has committed heresy, for the discharge petition is a "departure from normal procedures." The fact that it is specifically sanctioned by Rule XXVII of the House is not mentioned; the sophisticated congressman is expected to know that some things, though permissible, are simply not done. An additional obstacle to the success of a discharge petition is the exceptionally large number of signatures required: a majority of the *total House membership* must sign.

On the rare occasions when these inhibiting factors are over-

12 The Fair Labor Standards Act of 1938 and a government employees' salary increase (which postdated the Civil Rights Act of 1960).

..........Congress. **House of Representatives** No. ....

Motion to Discharge a Committee from the Consideration of a ....
(State whether bill, joint resolution, or resolution)

.............................., 19.....
(Date)

To the Clerk of the House of Representatives:

Pursuant to Clause 4 of Rule XXVII (see rule on page 7), I,

...., *move to discharge the*
(Name of Member)

Committee on ....
(Committee)

....

from the consideration of the ....
(Bill, joint resolution, or resolution)

H.R. ....; *H.J. Res.* ....; *H. Res.* ....
(Number, if a bill) (Number, if a joint resolution) (Number, if a resolution)

entitled, a ....
(Bill, joint resolution, or resolution) (Title)

....

....

which was referred to said committee ...., 19.....
(Date of reference)

in support of which motion the undersigned Members of the House of Representatives affix their signatures, to wit:

1.	12. ....
2.	13. ....
3.	14. ....
4.	15. ....
5.	16. ....
6.	17. ....
7.	18. ....
8.	19. ....
9.	20. ....
10.	21. ....
11.	22. ....

Sample of House discharge petition. Civil rights petition may not be reproduced, since it did not obtain 219 signatures required for official status.

come and a committee does find itself the target of a popular discharge petition, it often concludes that discretion is the better part of valor. With the petition lacking only a few signatures, the committee may decide to report out the bill and thus at least avoid the appearance of defeat. Whether it is a "legislative" committee or the Rules Committee that is involved, there is a practical reason for yielding. In the case of a legislative committee, it may not revise a bill that is forced from it through a discharge petition; if, on the other hand, the committee releases the bill voluntarily, an opportunity exists to introduce drastic changes before sending it to the House floor. As for the Rules Committee, a bill brought before the House without its consent is open to a wide variety of floor amendments and these may make it even more offensive to the committee than it was originally; if, however, the committee consents to release the bill, it can almost always persuade the House to restrict floor amendments or even ban them entirely.

It did not seem impossible that Celler's discharge petition would attract enough signatures to force the hand of the Rules Committee even if it did not win the support of a full 219 members of the House. With this in mind, Celler proceeded to introduce the necessary document.

CELLER FOUND IT ADVISABLE to resort to the identical discharge procedure in 1963. For although a moderate change in the Rules Committee had taken place two years earlier, the "reformed" body looked as unfriendly to civil rights as ever. This might have been expected, since the authors of the reform had been motivated by an interest in clearing the way not for civil rights but for economic legislation.

The 1961 reform had been tailored to the specifications of President-elect Kennedy. Confronted with the possibility that an unreconstructed Rules Committee might block significant elements of his legislative program, Mr. Kennedy had argued that the Democrats in the House should take steps to forestall this eventuality.

In obedience to his wishes, Speaker Rayburn got the House to add two Democrats and one Republican to the committee, thus increasing its membership from twelve to fifteen and relegating the conservative coalition to minority status. One of the new Democrats, however, was Carl Elliott of Alabama. The fact that Elliott was not hostile to liberal economic legislation meant that there might be a one-vote majority for such measures, but as a southerner the new member could hardly vote to clear civil rights legislation.

Accordingly, Chairman Smith felt free to drag his feet on the civil rights bill in 1963, much as he had done in 1959. Confronted with a familiar problem, Chairman Celler resorted to a familiar solution: the filing of a discharge petition.

Senate Judiciary Committee

AS H.R. 8601 painfully negotiated the obstacles of House procedure in 1959, a subcommittee on the other side of the Capitol was holding extensive hearings on the seventeen civil rights bills that had been introduced in the Senate. The Subcommittee on Constitutional Rights, a unit of the Senate Judiciary Committee, heard many of the same witnesses who had appeared before Celler. Although its hearings paralleled to a considerable extent those that had been conducted in the House, southern witnesses found the atmosphere here more to their liking. Congressman Rivers, who testified at both sets of hearings, supplied the explanation. "You are objective," he told the senators. "We do not have that over in our House." The South Carolinian's enthusiasm was understandable: three of the six Democrats on the Constitutional Rights Subcommittee were from the South.

If this southern representation was pleasing to the 39 opponents of civil rights who testified, it was a serious source of frustration for the chairman, Thomas C. Hennings, Jr. of Missouri. The conservative complexion of his subcommittee prevented him repeatedly from winning its approval for the liberal measures with which he was usually identified. When civil rights was the pending issue, it was a problem even to persuade the group to hold executive sessions so that legislation could be considered.

After public hearings had ended, Hennings complained that meetings often could not be held because an insufficient number of senators attended to provide the necessary quorum. In order for the subcommittee to transact business, five of its nine members were required to be present. Only three, however, could be depended upon to attend: Democrat John A. Carroll of Colorado; William Langer, a maverick Republican from North Dakota; and Hennings himself. Unless they were joined by the two remaining Republicans, the subcommittee was unable to act, for its three southern members would absent themselves and the ninth senator was recuperating from a stroke. On five separate occasions, therefore, Hennings found it impossible to assemble a quorum. In one instance, he had been compelled to postpone a subcommittee meeting for a week. The delay was caused by Sam J. Ervin, Jr. of North Carolina, who invoked a rule that prohibits a committee from meeting while the Senate is in session unless it obtains unanimous consent.[13] Even when the southerners did attend and thus made it possible for the subcommittee to meet, they usually had the votes to block any action they opposed.

In view of these factors, it was not surprising that Part III did not appear in the bill that the subcommittee approved. The only points that won acceptance were a fifteen-month extension of the Civil Rights Commission, and a requirement that voting records be held for three years and made available to federal agents for examination.

S. 2391, a clean bill limited to these two meager provisions,

---

[13] Ervin became chairman of the subcommittee in January 1961, four months after the death of Senator Hennings.

was submitted to the full Judiciary Committee on July 15, 1959. Although the subcommittee measure was even weaker than the one produced by the House Judiciary Committee, liberal senators hoped that its very innocuous character might help their cause by persuading the full Judiciary Committee to clear it for floor debate. If it was thus allowed to come before the Senate as a whole, it could—like H.R. 8601 in the House—provide the opportunity for amendments that would shape a civil rights bill worthy of the name.

The critical factor that would probably determine whether the liberals' strategy would work was the attitude of the Judiciary Committee and particularly of James O. Eastland, its chairman. The Mississippi senator was one of the most outspoken segregationists in Congress. Although he headed the committee that screened nominees to the Supreme Court, he openly preached defiance of that tribunal's decisions involving race relations. Nothing provoked his ire as easily as legislation to combat discrimination against the Negro.

SENIORITY SYSTEM

How had it come to pass that Eastland, who detested the very idea of civil rights, was chairman of the Judiciary Committee? The answer is provided by Congress' virtually inflexible seniority rule, which is used to distribute all chairmanships. In each house, the party with a majority of the seats is given a corresponding majority on all committees. Its members on each committee then unite as a matter of course to select as chairman whichever one of them has the longest record of continuous service on the committee. In the Eighty-sixth Congress, Eastland was the Democrat who met this criterion on the Judiciary Committee. Since the Democrats had a majority in the Senate, his selection as chairman was automatic. Ironically, this meant that a liberal voter in Illinois, for example, who had cast his ballot for Paul Douglas because of his civil rights stand, was—by helping the Democrats win a majority in the Senate—indirectly voting to make Eastland chairman of the Judiciary Committee.

Because the senority rule often results in the promotion of elderly members of Congress, it is sometimes derided as a "senility rule." [14] Apart from being unfair in many cases, this criticism is by no means the most significant one. In addition to apportioning some rewards for longevity, the seniority system always favors legislators who are assured of indefinite reelection for no better reason than that they repesent one-party states or districts. In the words of a leading political scientist, it puts power in the hands of those members of Congress who are "least aware of the problems of modern industrial society and least equipped to deal with them." It

> stacks the cards against those areas where competition for votes is the keenest, where the two-party system is the liveliest, where political currents run fresh and free. It stacks them in favor of the politically stagnant districts—those made "safe" for the incumbent by the poll tax and other restrictions on voting, by the monopolistic position of one party, by the ascendancy of a major interest group, by city or rural machines.[15]

When the Democrats are in power, the seniority system distributes most of the chairmanships to southerners, simply because the absence of serious Republican opposition in their states assures them of long tenure in office. Other Democrats, who must face competition, seldom retain their seats long enough to head a committee. Not surprisingly, therefore, about two-thirds of the committees in the Eighty-sixth Congress were chaired by southerners.

The chairman of a typical committee possesses enormous power. When he consents to call his committee into session, he decides what it shall discuss. It is he who schedules public hearings, invites witnesses, and presides. The employees of the committee are on his payroll; aside from giving him an opportunity to win political support by distributing lucrative jobs to influential constituents, this means that the important staff

---

[14] One writer mentions the case of Senator Arthur Capper of Kansas, who became chairman of the Committee on Agriculture and Forestry when he was eighty-one years old. "It was said of him at the time that he could hear no one and no one could hear him." Roland Young, *The American Congress* (New York: Harper, 1958), 71.

[15] James MacGregor Burns, *Congress on Trial* (New York: Harper, 1949), 59.

work is done by individuals who reflect his political philosophy. In 1946, the Legislative Reorganization Act increased the already imposing stature of chairmen. By reducing the roster of committees to one-third of what it had been, the new law enlarged the domain ruled by each chairman. Senator Eastland's committee, for example, was now given jurisdiction over fourteen major types of legislation.[16]

A chairman's power to obstruct legislation that he opposes is particularly important. Eastland employed this power skillfully against the civil rights bill. Soon after the Judiciary Committee began its deliberations on S. 2391, it became evident that he had no intention of allowing the bill to reach the floor. With his help, southerners kept the committee tied in knots. On two occasions, for example, Senator Olin D. Johnston of South Carolina forced postponement of action through parliamentary maneuvering. First, by requesting permission to file a minority report, he compelled the committee to mark time for one week. Then he won further delay by invoking an informal committee rule that any member may arbitrarily insist on a one-week moratorium.

The hour at which the committee met also gave Eastland an opportunity to forestall action. Since the Judiciary Committee normally did not convene until 10:30, only ninety minutes were available for transacting business, under the rule that committees could not meet after the Senate was called to order at noon unless they had obtained unanimous consent.[17] After opening the meeting, Eastland would at once give the floor by prearrangement to a loquacious southern colleague who would hold

---

16 But increasing the scope of a committee's jurisdiction often has led to the formation of subcommittees, and these impose a certain amount of restraint on the power of a chairman. This results from the tendency of subcommittees to become independent power centers. Although their recommendations on legislation may be rejected by the full committee, it is difficult to ignore them. Subcommittees may, among other things, hold hearings that help to influence public and congressional opinion in favor of a bill that the full committee may oppose.

17 Each of the two houses of Congress transacts a good deal of its business through unanimous consent. Yet the fact that almost anything may be done if no one objects creates a danger. Attendance on the floor is usually sparse, since senators and representatives have many obligations (such as committee meetings, conferences with officials of the executive branch, visits by constituents) to keep them away. As a consequence, there may sometimes be only a handful of

forth at length. Then, when the Senate had convened, the chairman would sustain a point of order forcing the committee to adjourn in obedience to the rule.

An additional boon to the southerners was the fact that the meetings of the Judiciary Committee take place on Monday,[18] when the Senate almost invariably meets (and occasionally turns its attention to the so-called Consent Calendar, which contains the noncontroversial bills that are often extremely important to individual congressmen). Thus the occasion never arose when the liberals on the Judiciary Committee could be sure that a meeting would last long enough to take action in behalf of civil rights. Apparently there was no shortage of garrulous senators who, at Eastland's bidding, would consume the time between 10:30 and noon. Their interests, moreover, ranged far and wide. Uncle Remus, *Aesop's Fables,* Old Testament prophets, and New Testament parables were all the subjects of oral readings, according to Senator Hennings.

ATTEMPTS TO DISLODGE BILL

The patience of the liberals was finally exhausted when Senator Johnston took the floor in the committee for what was billed as a speech of six or seven hours. Such an oration could consume several Mondays. Hennings gave up any hope that the Judiciary Committee would ever act. If civil rights was to come before the Senate, unorthodox methods seemed necessary. He therefore proceeded to file a series of civil rights measures as amendments to a bill pending before the Senate. Kenneth B. Keating of New York followed suit by offering similar amendments to a second bill.[19]

---

members present—and these few could transact business, since a quorum is always assumed to be present unless a point of order is made. To guard against whatever possibilities of partisan skulduggery this may open up, the Democratic and Republican leaders see to it that they are represented on the floor at all times by members ready to block unethical requests for unanimous consent.

[18] The southerners would have been still better off had there been no regular meeting day. Chairmen of committees in this category often can prevent action on legislation they oppose by simply neglecting to call meetings.

[19] The bill Keating selected as his vehicle dealt with peanuts, a subject of great importance to the South. He hoped that the southerners would accept civil rights rather than allow their region to suffer economically.

Hennings and Keating were not the only senators to exhibit impatience. Republicans Jacob K. Javits of New York and Clifford P. Case of New Jersey submitted a resolution to discharge the Judiciary Committee from further consideration of civil rights. Although such motions had been notably unsuccessful in the past, the two sponsors hoped that public pressure might enable this one to succeed.

The majority and minority leaders, however, cooperated to persuade liberals that they should abandon this insistence on immediate action. In September 1959, two months past the normal date of adjournment, Senator Johnson and Everett McKinley Dirksen, his Republican counterpart, abandoned hope of settling the civil rights issue during the first session of the Eighty-sixth Congress. But they promised solemnly that the Senate would begin consideration of civil rights by February 15, 1960, shortly after the second session convened. These were Johnson's words: "I serve notice on all members that on or about 12 o'clock on February 15, I anticipate that some senator will rise in his place and make a motion with regard to the general civil rights question." When Senator Javits sought assurance from the leader of his party that he would cooperate, Dirksen replied, in the mock-serious style that was his trademark: "If the Lord is willing and I am alive." Neither Johnson nor Dirksen explained how they proposed to honor their pledge, but the two men were as resourceful as they were powerful, and no one doubted that a way would be found.

UNLIKE THE PROCEDURE followed four years earlier, civil rights legislation in 1963 was referred not to a single committee in the Senate but to two separate committees. A strategic consideration was involved. The Judiciary Committee had never in its history released a civil rights bill voluntarily, and it was unlikely that this record would be altered as long as Senator Eastland remained as chairman of the committee. To help assure that a bill would be reported to the floor in spite of Mr. Eastland, the civil rights legislators worked out a justification for referring one of the titles (or sections) of the bill to a committee more favorably disposed toward the Negro than Judiciary.

This committee was the Commerce Committee, and the provisions of the bill that were referred to it concerned nondiscriminatory access to places of public accommodation. It was possible to argue that this subject lay within the jurisdiction of the Commerce Committee because the public accommodations section, as framed by the authors of the bill, was based on the Constitutional power of Congress "to regulate Commerce . . . among the several States. . . ."

There was another reason, too, for resorting to the commerce clause. The only other Constitutional provision which might have been invoked was the Fourteenth Amendment, and there was no certainty at all that the Supreme Court would be willing to overturn an 1883 decision that this Amendment did not authorize Congress to outlaw racial discrimination when carried on by private citizens. So the framers of the legislation chose what looked like a safer route. They took comfort from the knowledge that since 1937, when the Court stopped censoring federal economic legislation, not a single act of Congress purporting to be an exercise of the commerce power had been declared unconstitutional.

The Administration agreed that discrimination in places such as hotels and restaurants might well have an injurious effect on interstate commerce. Among other things, it argued, such discrimination "obstructs interstate travel and the sale of related goods and services [and] restricts business enterprises in their choice of locations for offices and plants, because of their inability to obtain the services of persons who do not wish to subject themselves to segregation and discrimination." There was thus a rational basis for pinning the public accommodations title to the commerce clause and referring that title to the Commerce Committee.

The hearings that the Commerce Committee proceeded to conduct were both comprehensive and businesslike. Over a period of 22 days, 47 witnesses were heard, 81 statements were received, and a record of more than 1500 pages was compiled. The committee chairman, Warren G. Magnuson (D., Wash.), made it clear that he would tolerate no obstructionism. At one point, a threat to hamstring the hearings was made by Senator Strom Thurmond of South Carolina (then a segregationist southern *Democrat* but soon to become a segregationist southern *Republican*). When it became known that Thurmond might deny the committee the unanimous consent needed to hold hearings during sessions of the Senate, Magnuson announced that in such an event he would schedule meetings for 8 o'clock in the morning so that there would be no delay in the committee's work.

By October 8, 1963, the Commerce Committee had concluded its hearings and was ready to report. The bill which it approved differed in certain respects from the one submitted by the House Judiciary Committee, but the important thing was that the leadership now had a vehicle available for bringing civil rights to the floor of the Senate.

The efficiency and dispatch with which the Commerce Committee worked contrasted sharply with what went on in the Judiciary Committee. Although Judiciary held hearings for eleven days, it heard only a single witness, Attorney General Kennedy. In addition, much of the eleven days was devoted not to listening to Mr. Kennedy *answer* questions but rather to listening to Senator Ervin *ask* questions. The Senator from North Carolina, who was considered something of an expert in constitutional law, brought to the hearings a stack of books three feet high, and for hour after excruciating hour questioned the Attorney General about their contents. Senator Keating made a vain attempt to accelerate the proceedings, suggesting to Eastland that night meetings be scheduled in order that the colloquy between Ervin and Kennedy might someday come to an end. But Eastland, evidently enthralled by Ervin's interrogation, turned down the suggestion and indicated that his committee was not going to spoil its perfect record of never voluntarily reporting a civil rights bill to the floor. Senate action in the first session of the Eighty-ninth Congress now seemed completely out of the question.

Extension of Civil Rights Commission

POSTPONEMENT of action in 1959 to the second session of Congress was not at all displeasing to Republican political strategists. The battle would now take place in an election year, with the Democrats fighting each other precisely when they were in greatest need of unity to capture the White House. Some liberals also thought that *they* perceived advantages in the delay. They reasoned that a southern threat to filibuster would not be too potent near the beginning of a session, for in the event that one did materialize there would still be enough time left to break it without sacrificing essential legislation. And they hoped also that political pressures for a strong bill would prove irresistible in a presidential election year.

But one action could not be delayed. The Civil Rights Commission, which had been created by the 1957 act, had to be given a new authorization or it would expire two months before Congress reconvened. There was, of course, the question of how to bypass the Judiciary Committee and bring an extension bill to the floor. Once the bipartisan congressional leadership agreed that it was desirable to extend the commission, however, obstacles that otherwise would have loomed large suddenly disappeared.

In the Senate, several unusual events took place. The Appropriations Committee approved, as an amendment to a high-priority foreign-aid bill, a provision to extend the commission's life for two years. Carl Hayden of Arizona, the Senate's President Pro Tempore,[20] moved to "suspend the rules"—the only way that legislation can be added to an appropriation bill. The necessary two-thirds vote was obtained handily, with only a single Republican joining seventeen southern Democrats in opposition. Then, on the question of adding the extension amendment to the main bill, approval came again, this time by a vote of 71–18.

Acceptance of the combination measure by the Senate meant that the two chambers had not adopted identical bills, since the one passed by the House was devoted purely to foreign aid. The bill containing the rider on the Civil Rights Commission was therefore returned to the House. The practice in such cases is to appoint a joint "conference committee" to produce a bill acceptable to both chambers. But to initiate the conference procedure, it was necessary to obtain either unanimous consent or the permission of the Rules Committee.[21] A request for unanimous consent was blocked by a southern congressman. The Rules Committee, however, yielded to leadership pressure and reported out a rule. The House accepted the rule by voice vote, sending the bill to conference. When the senators on the joint conference committee announced that they were irrevocably committed to the rider, the House voted to accept it, 221–81. President Eisenhower's signature on the bill meant that foreign aid had received a vote of

---

[20] When the Vice President of the United States, who is the presiding officer of the Senate, is absent, the President Pro Tem becomes the nominal head of the Senate. Usually, the President Pro Tem is the senior senator from his party. Such influence as he enjoys stems more from that fact than from the office itself.

[21] No longer does the Rules Committee play an important part in determining whether conferees should be appointed. At the opening of the Eighty-ninth Congress in 1965, the House adopted a change in its rules to permit a bill to be sent to conference by a simple majority vote on the floor. All that is now needed is for the Speaker to recognize a member to make an appropriate motion and for that motion to be approved.

confidence, and that the Civil Rights Commission had a new lease on life—as well as a $500,000 appropriation.[22]

EXTRAORDINARY PROCEDURES were again employed in 1963 to prevent the Civil Rights Commission from being forced to abandon its work. This time a twelve-month extension of the commission's life was added to a private relief bill in the Senate, with only southern Democrats voting in the negative. The measure to which the extension was attached was sent to the House, and there the Rules Committee was short-circuited through a motion to suspend the rules and adopt the Senate bill. The suspension was approved by far more than the necessary two-thirds vote; only a single northerner (Walter S. Baring, a Nevada Democrat) joined the Southerners in opposition.

REGISTRAR PLAN

The leadership's triumph in obtaining such speedy approval of the extension bill in 1959 was all the more impressive because it was won at a time when southerners were incensed at the commission for a report it had just published—the first since its creation. During its two-year lifetime, the commission had been engaged in studying voting complaints in the South, and discrimination in public education and housing in the entire nation. The report it issued on September 9, 1959 was encyclopedic. Its 668 pages contained a carefully documented exposure of racial discrimination, and a series of recommendations about how to eradicate it. The credentials of the com-

---

22 At least one congressman—John Dowdy of Texas—was unable to decide which aspect of the law made him angrier. "In my opinion," he said,

> the foreign aid provisions, in impoverishing America to build up socialism and communism in foreign lands, amount to treason; the extension of the so-called Civil Rights Commission, with the evident intent to overthrow the American way of life, amounts to tyranny. The Kremlin hierarchy would be proud to claim authoriship of this combination.

mission's members highlighted the importance of what they said. The chairman, a university president, had as his colleagues two former governors, two law school deans, and a distinguished Roman Catholic priest who was president of the University of Notre Dame.

Of the various sections contained in the report, the most striking concerned voting denials in the South. Basing its conclusions on data obtained largely through the hearings it had held in southern states, the commission charged that in sixteen predominantly Negro counties there were no registered voters but whites. In 49 other such counties, fewer than 5 per cent of the voting-age Negroes were registered. The commission asserted that apathy could not possibly explain such incredible statistics; the cause, rather, was racial discrimination. Nor did it believe that remedies provided by the Civil Rights Act of 1957 could overcome the abuses revealed by these figures. After groping for some more effective machinery, five of the six commissioners agreed to propose the appointment of temporary federal registrars.[23]

Under the plan that the commission advanced, any individual could submit to the President of the United States an affidavit alleging that he had been unable to register with state voting officials by reason of his race, color, or national origin. He would have to swear also that he believed himself qualified under state law. If the President received nine or more such complaints from a single county, he would refer them to the Civil Rights Commission for verification. After an investigation had weeded out any petitions that might be lacking in merit, the President would designate a federal officer or employee in the area to act as a temporary voting registrar.

The registrar would respect any qualifications that state law imposed on registration. Administering with an even hand the

---

[23] The only dissent from this recommendation came from Commissioner John S. Battle, former governor of Virginia. Battle feared that registrar legislation would "place in the hands of the federal government a vital part of the election process so jealously guarded and carefully preserved to the states by the Founding Fathers."

state's own standards, he would issue registration certificates conferring the right to vote on disfranchised persons, but only in federal elections. He would continue to serve until the President determined that his services were no longer needed.

END OF FIRST SESSION

The commission's report was issued during the closing days of the congressional session, with House and Senate driving hard toward adjournment and most members interested in little else.[24] That was why even the registrar proposal, which at a later date was to become the object of microscopic examination, was now virtually ignored, except by southerners, who were quick to criticize it. Six days after the recommendations were published, Congress agreed to renew the commission's mandate and was finally able to adjourn.

When at last the end of the session came, it was 6:24 A.M. and the visitors' galleries were almost empty. That was probably just as well, for the scene to which the few onlookers were treated could not have enhanced their respect for Congress. A reporter described "groggy members . . . routed from their offices" and "over-extended celebrants . . . herded to the floor" for the final roll call votes.[25]

As the session ended, supporters of civil rights had little more than hope to buoy their spirits. Not a single significant barrier to the passage of a bill had yet been surmounted. In the House, there was still the Rules Committee to be vanquished or circumvented. In the Senate, it would be difficult to coax a bill from the Judiciary Committee and, if this improbable event did occur, it might prove impossible to overcome the filibuster that could be expected. The administration seemed to consider civil rights far down in its order of priorities. President Eisenhower

---

24 One reason for the frantic haste to adjourn was the desire on the part of the congressional leaders to flee Washington before the scheduled arrival of Soviet Premier Nikita S. Khrushchev. They wanted to avoid the predicament of having to choose between snubbing him and inviting him to address a joint session.

25 Russell Baker, *The New York Times* (September 16, 1959, Late City Edition), 23.

had never personally endorsed the Supreme Court's school segregation decisions, and there were recurrent rumors that this was so because he actually disagreed with them. Only the most wildly optimistic liberal could dream that a strong civil rights bill would be enacted in 1960.

FOUR YEARS LATER, shortly before the first session of the Eighty-eighth Congress ended, an event occurred that seemed to demand a complete reassessment of the civil rights problem—and of the very future of American society, for that matter: the assassination of President Kennedy. That event stimulated an agonizing national self-examination. Did the mindless murder of a President epitomize the violent attitudes and violent actions that had come to permeate American life? Might there be a meaningful connection between the violence in which the assassin of the President had placed his trust and the violence that the nation had so long tolerated against the Negro minority?

There was irony in the fact that such questions were being asked during the first days of the Johnson Administration, because the man who was now President had never bothered to conceal his contempt for those who believed that racial discrimination could only be eradicated through strong federal legislation. Yet the thinking of Lyndon Johnson had been undergoing a transformation even before that day in Dallas. Defeat in his fight for the presidential nomination in 1960 had made Mr. Johnson wonder whether he had really done enough to dispel the popular impression that he was just another parochial southerner. And the same events in Birmingham that had shaken Mr. Kennedy's faith in gradualism had also shattered his own assumption that the civil rights problem could wait.

A scant five days after the assassination, the nation learned where civil rights now stood on the Johnson agenda. In a funereal address to a joint session of Congress, the new President said: ". . . No memorial oration or eulogy could more eloquently honor President Kennedy's memory than the earliest possible passage of the civil rights bill for which he fought so long." Mr. Johnson emphasized the importance he attached to the bill by giving it first place on his "must" list. He also emphasized it through the emphatic language he employed. "We have talked long enough in this country about equal rights," he said. "We have talked for one hundred years or more. It is time now to write the next chapter—and to write it in the books of law. I urge you . . . to enact a civil rights law so that we can move forward to eliminate from this nation every trace of discrimination and oppression that is based upon race or color."

Mr. Johnson's plea was greeted with stormy applause by both Democrats and Republicans. Suddenly the question of who would profit politically from the passage of a bill seemed of little significance, and the cracks that had begun to appear in the united front of the two parties disappeared. The national feeling of bereavement and shame and guilt had produced a wave of sympathy for the Kennedy legislative program. That factor, combined with the presence in the White House of a master legislative strategist who could not afford to look like just another southerner, significantly improved the prospects for a strong civil rights bill.

Advice for Congress

WHEN the Eighty-sixth Congress convened for its second session on January 6, 1960, two significant new factors were in the foreground of the civil rights situation: the imminence of the presidential election, and the impact of the report by the Civil Rights Commission. One month later, an entirely new quantity was injected. That was the phenomenon of the lunchcounter "sit-ins."

The first of these demonstrations took place on February 1. Four Negro students from a North Carolina college entered a Woolworth five-and-dime store in Greensboro and seated themselves at the lunchcounter. After their request for service was ignored, they remained seated for one hour. This simple incident provided the inspiration for many other young Negroes in various parts of the South to dramatize their protest against racial exclusion. Everywhere the demonstrators carefully shunned violence, even when this meant submitting to insults and blows. This policy was in harmony with the philosophical doctrines of Reverend Martin Luther King, Jr., who had led a boycott against segregated buses in Montgomery, Ala., and who counseled nonviolent struggle against all forms of racial discrimination.

If the practice of turning the other cheek was the most remarkable aspect of the sit-ins, their deeper significance lay elsewhere. The recourse to direct action indicated a growing conviction on the part of the new Negro in the South [26] that court procedures offered no effective remedy for segregation. Unlike his ancestors, he would not be willing to wait patiently for progress that might never come. The lesson that the sit-in movement contained for Congress was obvious. If the federal government persisted in denying the Negro effective legal tools, direct action might become the rule rather than the exception.

In this atmosphere of heightened interest in civil rights, President Eisenhower delivered his State of the Union mes-

---

[26] Roy Wilkins, executive secretary of the NAACP, has written this desecription of the difference between the old and the new generations:

> The soothing double-talk handed to Aunt Mandy and Uncle Jim falls on the deaf and scornful ears of today's Tom, Dick, and Harry. These latter have traveled far from the home county; tens of thousands have been off to war and seen far places; thousands more have gone to school under the G.I. Bill; they have radios and television sets; they read newspapers, magazines, and books. That is why the Montgomery bus protest lasted one year instead of five days as predicted by local whites who "knew" their Negroes.

sage. Although his reaction to the report of the Civil Rights Commission had been eagerly awaited, Mr. Eisenhower chose to say little. The entire subject of civil rights occupied a mere 48 words in a message one hundred times as long. This was the President's statement:

> Early in your last session, I recommended legislation which would help eliminate several practices discriminating against the basic rights of Americans. The Commission on Civil Rights has developed additional constructive recommendations. I hope that these will be among the matters to be seriously considered in the current session.

The President had not singled out any particular recommendations of the commission that he wanted "seriously considered," nor had he explicitly endorsed a single recommendation made by the commission. An editorial in *The New York Times* complained that his "almost casual treatment" of the civil rights question would "not make the fight for an effective . . . bill this session any easier."

THERE WERE NO such complaints when President Johnson delivered *his* first State of the Union message. Just as he had done in his initial address to Congress soon after the assassination, the new President gave top priority to civil rights. "Let this session of Congress be known as the session which did more for civil rights than the last hundred sessions combined," he said.

The contrast between the old Johnson and the new Johnson could not have been greater. As Majority Leader, Mr. Johnson had never tired of berating those who felt that gradual progress toward racial equality was insufficient. Now, as President of the United States at a time when large-scale racial violence threatened to erupt, he saw things differently. "As far as the writ of federal law will run," he said, "we must abolish not some but all racial discrimination." The former senator pulled out all the stops. "Today," he said, "Americans of all races stand side by side in Berlin and Viet Nam. They died side by side in Korea. Surely they can work and eat and travel side by side in their own country." Prolonged applause greeted these words. Mr. Johnson's artless emotionalism had struck a responsive chord in men whose makeup he knew well.

REGISTRARS

The members of Congress were unable to tell from Mr. Eisenhower's State of the Union address in 1960 how the President felt about the proposal by the Civil Rights Commission that federal registrars be authorized. A press conference the following week, however, left little doubt on this point. In response to a question about the commission's proposal, Mr. Eisenhower declared: "I don't even know whether it is constitutional." The President explained that he did not want to foreclose study of this or any other idea; he merely meant that Congress would do well to concentrate on the package of civil rights measures he had submitted in 1959.[27] But even before his press conference, Justice Department officials had privately made clear that they would not be displeased if the registrar plan could be swept under a rug. They claimed to have already discovered some defects. Besides, they said, the commission plan—or any

---

27 This was the President's verbatim response:

I don't know—as a matter of fact, I don't even know whether it is constitutional. What I am saying is, or what the Commissioners said, this was one plan that they thought might have some measure of validity, and, therefore, they wanted to study it. Now, the way I feel about this civil rights, we have one bill that was put in last year in which extensive hearings have been heard—had; and I should like to see the Congress act decisively on this particular proposal, and such other proposals made as —that now become almost controversial from the moment that they are presented—would not enter into the proposal or to the process of examining and passing the bill that was already put before the Congress.

Question. You mean——

The President. You see, I don't have any—what I am trying to get at is, I have no objection to the study of the others. As a matter of fact, I want to study them because I would like to see what everybody thinks about it. My big problem is, though, let's get this bill already proposed on which they have had hearings, let's get that acted on.

other addition to the administration's civil rights program—might endanger the whole package.

The President's opposition to the registrar idea had dealt a sharp blow to its prospects. Nonetheless, bills embodying the proposal were introduced and committee hearings held in both the House and the Senate. The forum in the House was again Congressman Celler's Judiciary Committee. In the upper chamber, however, Senator Hennings, who was strongly for civil rights, was now in full charge. Although the 1959 hearings, too, had been conducted by Hennings, he was then acting in a subordinate capacity—as chairman of a subcommittee under Eastland. Now, in sharp contrast, a full committee that he chaired was conducting the hearings. This change had come about because the registrar bill dealt specifically with voting. Ordinarily, civil rights legislation is referred to the Judiciary Committee, but bills relating to federal elections are placed in a different category by the rules of the Senate. These go to the Committee on Rules and Administration.[28]

As chairman of that committee, Senator Hennings decided to hold early hearings on the proposal for registrars. There was scant hope that he could persuade his colleagues on the committee to report out a registrar bill, but the hearings would at least prevent southerners from claiming, if the plan ever reached the floor, that the idea of registrars had never received detailed study by a full committee.

One of the most important witnesses who testified before the Hennings committee was Robert G. Storey, vice-chairman of the Civil Rights Commission. He was subjected to close questioning by Senator Ervin.[29] Under the registrar scheme, said the North Carolina senator, the President would be "put under

---

28 The assignment of the registrar bill to the Committee on Rules and Administration was not made without protest. Senator Johnston of South Carolina pointedly reminded the Senate of the existence of an appropriate Judiciary subcommittee (Constitutional Rights).

29 The senator was not a member of the Committee on Rules and Administration. But Senator Jordan, his fellow North Carolinian and the only southerner on the committee, had invited him to question Dr. Storey. Ervin was regarded in the South as a constitutional authority.

the command, in a sense," of Dr. Storey's agency. The commission, he explained, could constrain the Chief Executive to appoint a registrar at any time, as long as it felt that discrimination was keeping the ballot from qualified persons. Ervin predicted that some registrars would be carpetbaggers and that due process of law would be denied to state election officials.

Dr. Storey, however, would not be drawn into a discussion of particulars. He contented himself with a defense of the registrar idea in principle. "All we want to do," he said, "is to recommend that the Congress take appropriate action to do away with the evils that we have found in our investigation."

Nine senators testified at the hearings. Perhaps the most eloquent defense of the registrar proposal came from Senator Hubert H. Humphrey of Minnesota, who was soon to challenge Senator John F. Kennedy for the Democratic presidential nomination and was later to become Vice President of the United States. Humphrey said acidly:

> This government looks very puny, very weak, and rather immoral, enforcing small statutes upon citizens for minor breaches of the law when [it] has not the moral courage apparently to even protect constitutional rights. I sometimes wonder if we have the same enthusiasm for a man's right to vote that we do in collecting taxes.

Senator Herman Talmadge of Georgia spoke for the opposing viewpoint with even greater passion. He declared:

> We can keep our country free if we keep our elections free. We cannot keep our elections free if the electorate is to be determined by registration officials who owe their allegiance to a President who owes his allegiance to a political party which elected him. To those who think otherwise, I would point out the stark fact of history that Adolf Hitler's dictatorship became absolute when he was given power to appoint members of the German Reichstag.

Despite the heat generated by both sides, the committee was reluctant to make a decision without first receiving testimony from Attorney General Rogers. Before the opening of the hearings, Rogers had been invited by Hennings to appear at the earliest opportunity, for it was "most important" that his views be presented. The Attorney General, however, had been obliged to keep the committee waiting for three weeks, while an administration alternative to the register proposal was being formulated. Soon after the substitute plan had been unveiled, he made his appearance.

REFEREES

In his testimony before the Hennings committee, Rogers announced that the Department of Justice favored a system of "voting referees" in preference to the commission's idea of federal registrars. The difference between the two plans concerned more than just nomenclature. The commission had contemplated an exclusively administrative proceeding, which would not require action by the courts. But the Attorney General would involve the federal judiciary in two ways: there would have to be a successful legal action under the 1957 Civil Rights Act before the referee section could be invoked; and the referees, who would register qualified Negroes, would be appointed by judges.

In a statement issued when the referee proposal was released, Rogers pointed out that the plan would cover elections of both state and federal officials, while the registrar proposals were directed only at national elections. He expressed the fear that the commission's method might lead to "a system of 'separate and unequal' voting, with whites registering at one place and voting in all elections, and Negroes registering in another and attempting to vote in national elections." He also considered it deplorable that adoption of the registrar plan would leave state elections unprotected. This would have to be the case, he said, because the constitutional basis of the plan was Article I, Section 4,[30] which gives Congress power only over *federal* elections. The referee machinery, on the other hand, was "a plainly appropriate method of enforcing the Fifteenth

---

[30] "The Times, Places and Manner of holding Elections for Senators and Representatives shall be prescribed in each State by the Legislature thereof; but the Congress may at any time by Law make or alter such Regulations, except as to the Places of chusing [*sic*] Senators."

Amendment,"[31] which prohibits *any* infringement of the right to vote on the ground of race or color. Under this amendment, Rogers said, there was no question about the power of the federal government to intervene in state elections, as long as there had been a judicial determination that the Constitution had been violated. Only the referee plan supplied the necessary court proceeding.

DOUBTS EXPRESSED

But some members of Congress were troubled by precisely the court proceedings that the referee plan entailed. Were they not so complex that many Negroes would hesitate to use them? Was it fair that a man who merely wanted to vote should have to pick his way through a legal jungle?

Despite these reservations about referees, the plan was incorporated into a bill, H.R. 10065, which Representative McCulloch, the ranking Republican on the Judiciary Committee, agreed to sponsor. He planned to offer it on the House floor as an amendment to H.R. 8601, the measure that was still imprisoned in the Rules Committee.

Supporters of civil rights were dismayed at the possibility that a deadlock might develop between the supporters of the registrar and referee proposals. If the civil rights camp became embroiled in controversy, they feared, the results might be disastrous. In an effort to prevent this from happening, an off-the-record strategy meeting of persons promoting civil rights legislation was held. When *The New York Times* reported that a staff member of the Civil Rights Commission had attended, Senator Talmadge of Georgia erupted with anger. In a letter to each member of the commission, he wrote:

> It is inconceivable that a member of the staff . . . could be meeting with advocates of stronger civil rights proposals and advising them as to their strategy. Such action is tantamount to a

---

[31] "The right of citizens of the United States to vote shall not be denied or abridged by the United States or by any State on account of race, color, or previous condition of servitude. The Congress shall have power to enforce this article by appropriate legislation."

trial judge and members of a jury empaneled to try cases meeting with prosecution witnesses to make certain of a conviction in a pending case.

The staff director of the commission, Gordon M. Tiffany, promptly revealed that he himself had attended the conference, along with two assistants. He denied any impropriety since, he said, the discussion had never gone beyond "analysis and criticism of pending measures" while he was present. Undoubtedly, however, the very fact that he had attended the meeting indicated the extent to which the commission and its staff were intent on trying to reconcile the rival proposals.

Such a reconcilation was especially difficult to accomplish because the atmosphere was suffused with partisan politics. Some Republicans felt wedded to the referee plan simply because the administration had devised it. Apart from Celler, who had been quick to endorse the idea of referees, most Democrats wanted no part of civil rights legislation written in the White House. Passage of a "Republican bill" could do wonders for the Grand Old Party, especially in the pivotal northern states.[32]

Both the registrar plan and the referee plan, as well as additional voting proposals and scores of bills that dealt with other aspects of the civil rights problem, were now before congressional committees. There was still the matter of getting them to the floor. In the House, the laborious solicitation of signatures on the discharge petition went on. In the Senate, all eyes were on Lyndon Johnson, who had given his word that by February 15 the debate would begin. As his self-imposed deadline approached, the majority leader continued to keep his own counsel as to how he proposed to honor his pledge. Even on the morning of the red-letter day, there was still no indication of exactly what action he planned to take.

32 The Rogers plan troubled Democrats also because of fear that any prestige gained by the Attorney General might rub off on his close friend, Vice President Nixon, who was the leading candidate for the Republican presidential nomination.

Senate Debate Opens

ON FEBRUARY 15, the Senate was called to order in perfectly routine fashion. The chaplain, Reverend Frederick Brown Harris, mixed his customary quota of metaphors in his opening prayer.[33] As usual, the journal of the previous day was approved and its reading dispensed with. And, according to custom, the Majority Leader took the floor. There was nothing even remotely unusual in what he said. Here is how the *Congressional Record* reports the proceedings at this point:

> MR. JOHNSON of Texas. Mr. President, I ask unanimous consent that the Senate proceed to the consideration of Calendar No. 924, House Bill 8315.
> THE PRESIDENT PRO TEMPORE. The Bill will be stated by title, for the information of the Senate.
> THE LEGISLATIVE CLERK. A Bill (H.R. 8315) to authorize the Secretary of the Army to lease a portion of Fort Crowder, Mo., to Stella reorganized schools R-I, Mo.
> THE PRESIDENT PRO TEMPORE. Is there objection to the request for the present consideration of the Bill?
> There being no objection, the Senate proceeded to consider the Bill, which had been reported from the Committee on Armed Services, with an amendment.

Senators did not realize that the inconsequential bill they had just agreed to consider had been earmarked for great things. Johnson soon revealed what was in store. He explained:

> Because there is, as yet, no civil rights legislation on the Senate Calendar, this bill has been selected as the one on which, in fulfillment of the . . . pledge of last year, to begin the discussion of civil rights proposals in this chamber.
> The bill is open to amendment. I hope all interested senators will

---

[33] "The potent power of love can redeem and heal all the faults and flaws that spoil life's perfect melody." "Give us to see that harbored hate and bitterness always rob life of its joy and beauty, and that as we surrender to them they shrink our very souls."

offer, in a spirit of constructive, responsible, and nonpartisan dedication to human rights, the proposals they believe will best serve the ends of protecting the constitutional rights of American citizens.

Promptly, Dirksen introduced as an amendment to the Stella bill the seven-point civil rights program that had been requested by the President in 1959, as well as the referee plan. At long last, a civil rights bill was on the Senate floor.

Johnson and Dirksen had accomplished this feat by taking advantage of the fact that amendments in the Senate, as contrasted with those offered in the House, need not be germane to the subject matter of the bill they seek to modify. On Johnson's motion, the sprinkling of senators on the floor had agreed unanimously that they would discuss a House-passed bill dealing with one topic. Now they learned that they would really be talking about something quite different.

Senators were especially caught off-guard by the fact that the Stella bill was not even distantly related to civil rights. It was designed to permit the leasing of an unused officers club as a temporary replacement for a country school that had been destroyed by fire. So noncontroversial was it that the vote supporting it in the House had been unanimous.

Those familiar with congressional procedure knew it was no accident that Johnson had selected a bill already approved by the House. His maneuver was designed to counter the Rules Committee's obstruction in the House, as well as the Judiciary Committee's tactics in the Senate. Since amendments added by the Senate to a House-passed bill go directly to the House floor, the civil rights provisions—technically only a series of amendments to the Stella bill—would not have to be funneled through the Rules Committee once they had been adopted by the Senate.

The ingeniousness of the Johnson tactic infuriated the southern Democrats. Their acknowledged leader, Richard Russell of Georgia, was on his feet at once to accuse Johnson of "lynching . . . orderly procedure in the Senate." He said angrily: "We are the only minority which is not supposed to have any rights whatsoever." Bracing himself for the wide variety of civil rights amendments in prospect, the southerner complained that no

LEASING OF PORTION OF FORT CROWDER, MO.

The PRESIDING OFFICER. Under the unanimous-consent agreement, House bill 8315 is laid before the Senate.

The Senate resumed the consideration of the bill (H.R. 8315) to authorize the Secretary of the Army to lease a portion of Fort Crowder, Mo., to Stella Reorganized Schools R-I, Missouri.

The PRESIDING OFFICER. The question is on agreeing to the committee amendment.

Mr. JOHNSON of Texas. Mr. President, the unfinished business now before the Senate, H.R. 8315, relates to the leasing of a portion of Camp Crowder to a school district in Missouri.

Because there is, as yet, no civil rights legislation on the Senate Calendar, this bill has been selected as the one on which, in fulfillment of the Senate's pledge of last year, to begin the discussion of civil rights proposal in this Chamber.

The bill is open to amendment. I hope all interested Senators will offer, in a spirit of constructive, responsible, and nonpartisan dedication to human rights, the proposals they believe will best serve the ends of protecting the constitutional rights of American citizens.

Although it has brought me some criticism from both sides, I still look with humble satisfaction on my participation in the passage of the Civil Rights Act of 1957. I believed then, and I believe now, that action on that measure represented the Congress in its best traditions.

We are again called upon to act in this difficult and important field. I have confidence in the Senate. I believe the Senate will, in due time, act constructively, and in accord with a collective desire to do what is right.

Mr. DIRKSEN. Mr. President, I submit an amendment to the pending bill.

The PRESIDING OFFICER. The Chair is advised that the committee amendment should be disposed of before any other amendment is considered. The question is on agreeing to the committee amendment.

Mr. RUSSELL. Mr. President, the procedure here today is rather remarkable. Here we have a bill that relates to a school district in the State of Missouri and the leasing for a period of 2 years of some Army facilities to be used for a schoolhouse. The bill is a very minor and a modest one. But, Mr. President, I understand that this minor bill has been selected as the vehicle for the outpouring of every conceivable form of proposed legislation touching either directly or indirectly on the field which euphemistically is labeled "civil rights."

Mr. President, it so happens that I am honored to preside over the Senate Committee on Armed Services. This bill was reported by that committee. I wish to say that at the time when the committee deliberated on the bill, we had not the slightest inkling that this modest local bill, of interest to the good people of this small community in Missouri, would be used as the vehicle for bringing into this Chamber the burning, controversial question of civil rights. Nor do I believe, Mr. President, that when the people of Fort Crowder, Mo., launched this measure on the legislative seas, they had the slightest suspicion that their efforts to provide for the education of the young people of their community would be seized upon as an opportunity to provoke this discussion.

So, Mr. President, this is a most remarkable procedure.

I rise to protest action of this sort. In connection with the pending bill it cannot correctly be said that the distinguished senior Senator from Mississippi [Mr. EASTLAND], who presides over the Judiciary Committee, had prevented the Senate from taking action. It is true that no bill on this subject had been reported by the Judiciary Committee; but there are on the Calendar bills which have come from the Senate Judiciary Committee. I prefer that one of those bills be used, rather than one reported from the committee over which I am privileged to preside.

But, in addition, the Committee on Rules and Administration, which is presided over by the Senator from Missouri [Mr. HENNINGS], concluded hearings on February 5 on the proposed Federal voting registrar and referee legislation which has been proposed to take over and administer the laws of the several States of the Union with respect to voting. That committee has not reported a bill; but certainly no one who is familiar with the record of the Senator from Missouri would charge him with being derelict in any way in giving the Senate a proper vehicle for discussing the so-called and euphemistically entitled "civil rights legislation."

Mr. President, we are engrossed in the present debate because last year the statement was made that on the 15th day of February, 1960—with or without any hearings, with or without any committee report, whether it conformed and comported with orderly procedure or not—the Senate would proceed to a discussion of what is called civil rights legislation.

Mr. President, in all of this controversy and discussion we have heard a great deal about minorities. The only minority in the Senate that is considered not to have any rights at all is the group of Southern Democrats that has been undertaking to protect its people and the rights of its States.

In this case we are not following orderly procedure. Instead, we are confronted with this tiny catchall basket and are told: "Flood it with all your civil rights amendments, whatever they may be."

This morning I heard a distinguished Senator say on this floor that we must do something about the bombings of edifices, and that such a measure would be in the category of civil rights legislation. Mr. President, I favor taking action in regard to the bombing of edifices, whether public or private; but I do not regard a measure to deal with that subject as having anything to do with civil rights legislation.

It has become popular in this country—and certain groups favor it—to lump together as "civil rights" all kind of legislation to invade the schoolhouses of the Southern States, to take over the voting privileges of the people of the Southern States, to bring all kinds of harassment against the 40 million people who happen to live in the South—all on the ground that this is "civil rights."

Mr. MORSE. Mr. President, will the Senator from Georgia yield?

Mr. RUSSELL. Yes, Mr. President, I yield to the Senator from Oregon.

Mr. MORSE. Am I to understand that House bill 8315, Calendar No. 924, the pending business, refers to a request for approval of a lease of a portion of Fort Crowder, Mo., for property to be used as a public school building in that area?

Mr. RUSSELL. That is correct. I assumed that perhaps the Morse formula was involved. I saw that the distinguished Senator from Oregon had the speaking stand on his desk and was well fortified with many papers. I had assumed that the bill conformed with the Morse formula. But I observe that the Senator from Oregon had information—which was not available to me—that the bill was to be used as a catchall for proposals dealing with the so-called question of civil rights.

Mr. MORSE. I believe the Senator from Georgia will be pleased and surprised to learn that for the first time I am becoming aware of the proposed procedure in the Senate. I had no idea that Calendar No. 924, House bill 8315, was to be used as a springboard prior to a long swim in the sea of civil rights.

I wish to understand clearly the proposed procedure, because if that is the situation, then I rise to protest it. I do not believe this little bill, which seeks to make available to a school district some school facilities which apparently are very much needed by that school district, should be used as the basis for a whole series of riders on civil rights.

Mr. RUSSELL. I am glad to find that the Senator's interest extends to the tiny part of the population in Fort Crowder, Mo., which is interested in the passage of this bill. I hope that his interest will also extend to the position of those of us who desire to know exactly what we are to be confronted with—whether it is proposed to boil us in oil, or to burn us at the stake, or to fricassee us on some new kind of rack or wheel, or simply to burn off several inches of our bodies.

Mr. MORSE. If the Senator from Georgia will yield further, let me say that I favor the passage of House bill 8315, without any civil rights amendment or rider. I am opposed to legislation by rider. I believe that the people of this school district are entitled to have this bill voted either up or down by the Senate, without the raising of a civil rights issue in connection with it, unless someone can show me that a civil rights proposal is germane to the provisions of this bill. That has not been brought out yet. Then I am for the Senate of the United States bringing up a civil rights bill and proceeding to use a civil rights bill as the process for

Page of Congressional Record: *Bill is brought before Senate in 1960.*

one could tell in advance the details of what was to be debated, for the bills had not even been printed yet. This meant, he said, that the South did not know

> . . . whether it is proposed to boil us in oil, or to burn us at the stake, or to fricassee us on some new kind of rack or wheel, or simply to burn off several inches of our bodies. . . . We do not know whether we will be sandbagged or kicked or gagged or bound or what. . . .

THE SENATOR FROM OREGON

Russell received strong support from other southerners. But assistance was forthcoming also from one somewhat surprising source. The unpredictable Wayne Morse of Oregon, always ready to battle for civil rights, demonstrated that he was no less interested in preserving what he considered proper procedures. "I am opposed to legislation by rider," he announced. As an alternative, Morse offered a discharge motion that would bring to an end the smothering of the civil rights bills by the Judiciary Committee and the Committee on Rules and Administration. The Oregon senator declared that Johnson was subjecting the two committees to disorderly procedures. Even the Judiciary Committee, he said, although it was obviously engaging in dilatory tactics on civil rights, deserved to be protected from erosion of its legitimate functions. Upon hearing this, Johnson exploded. Morse's idea of the way to "protect" the Judiciary Committee was a motion that would "kick the committee in the teeth," he charged. "I know of no more disorderly procedure." [34]

Johnson's maneuver regarding the Stella bill, however, was strongly supported by Senator Dirksen, obviously as the result of an agreement that had been worked out in advance. The

---

[34] Disorderly or not, the Senate's discharge procedure is certainly an unwieldy tool in the face of determined opposition. A student of Senate rules has estimated that use of the discharge method would mean a minimum of five to eight weeks for the enactment of a civil rights bill, "even if there were 64 votes in support of action at every stage. . . ." Howard E. Schuman, "Senate Rules and the Civil Rights Bill: A Case Study," *American Political Science Review,* LI (December 1957), 964.

Minority Leader admitted that unorthodox tactics were being employed, but he argued that they were necessary, and he was willing to share with Johnson "any castigation or blame." With the two leaders working together, the opposition was doomed. Morse's resolution to discharge the Judiciary Committee was supported by only three other senators, and his motion regarding the other committee was defeated on a voice vote. An effort by Russell to delay consideration of civil rights for a week won support from only five senators outside the South (Morse and four Republicans); it was rejected, 61–28. Johnson told his fellow senators, "I think we have made a good deal of progress today." Although the southerners were threatening a filibuster, it was pleasing to believe that the Majority Leader was right.

IN 1964, THE SENATE LEADERSHIP made no effort to bring civil rights to the floor until after the House had approved a modified version of the bill reported by its Judiciary Committee, for fear that an earlier fight could poison the atmosphere in which the question of tax reduction would be debated. But a second consideration was also involved. Under the rules of the Senate, a bill that comes from the House can be intercepted at the door of the Senate chamber and placed directly on the calendar instead of first being referred to committee. Thus, once the House had acted on civil rights, a simple and effective procedure would be available for circumventing the Judiciary Committee.

When the House bill finally reached the Senate, Majority Leader Mansfield made the motion to make use of that procedure. His action did not go unchallenged. Senator Russell of Georgia, the leader of the southern bloc, was quick to object (as he had also done during the battle over civil rights in 1957) that a more recent rule took precedence over the one under which Mansfield wanted the Senate to proceed. Russell was referring to the rule specifying the appropriate committees to which bills on various subjects were to go. He interpreted this rule as requiring that all bills—even those already passed by the House—must be sent to some committee before being brought to the floor.

But Mansfield advanced a completely different interpretation of the newer rule. There had been no intention, he said, to supersede the procedure allowing committees to be bypassed when the Senate has before it a bill already accepted in the House. On the contrary, the rule was only meant to designate the proper committee to which a bill on a particular subject should be referred *if the Senate desired to refer it to committee at all.* By a vote of 54 to 37, the Senate decided to accept Mansfield's interpretation.

Just as he had done in 1960, Senator Morse sided with the southerners in objecting to the bypassing of the Judiciary Committee. Even if it was *legal* to ignore the committee, he said, it was far from *wise.* For only if the committee held hearings would the courts later have the benefit of a full legislative record on which to base their interpretation of the law that emerged. The Oregon Senator recognized that the committee might refuse to release the bill, but he offered a motion that contained a simple solution to that problem: the Senate should instruct the committee to report the measure to the floor within ten days. The Morse motion, however, was defeated.

Senator Mansfield was instrumental in engineering its defeat. Nevertheless, he felt no sense of triumph, since he, too, had wanted committee hearings to be held in the Senate. Even before Morse presented his motion, Mansfield himself had asked for referral to the Judiciary Committee, but with two firm instructions: first, the bill was to be reported back within one week; and, second, the committee was neither to propose amendments nor make recommendations. The Mansfield suggestion, requiring unanimous consent, was blocked by two senators with quite different motives: Jacob K. Javits (R., N.Y.), who did not want to dignify the Judiciary Committee by referring the bill to it at all; and Chairman Eastland, who did not want the Senate to insult the committee by tying its hands so firmly with instructions.

But even if the bill was not to go to the Judiciary Committee, it had no guaranty at all of clear sailing in the Senate. The greatest threat still lay ahead. In 1964, as in 1960, the filibuster was available to those senators from the South who were irreconcilable.

Filibusters and Their Antidotes

THE FILIBUSTER is the best known—and perhaps the least understood—activity of the United States Senate. What the word conjures up in the minds of many is an interminable speech on an irrelevant subject: Huey Long, for example, teaching his colleagues how to prepare "potlikker" (which he defined as "the residue that remains from the commingling, heating, and evaporation—anyway, it's in the bottom of the pot"); or a senator reading from the Manhattan telephone directory, or from the Bible, or from the preceding day's *Congressional Record*. Yet there has been no such episode in years. Today a senator participating in a filibuster is even more careful to adhere to the subject than he is on other, less publicized occasions. He does not want to be ridiculed for childishly wasting the Senate's time.

Others who try to define a filibuster picture it as a marathon oratorical effort by a single senator whose physical condition permits him to stand on the Senate floor for a day and a night, subjecting his colleagues to the only type of cruel and unusual punishment that the Constitution does not proscribe.[35] This type of filibuster, however, represents no serious problem for the Senate, because mere waiting will suffice to overcome it. Of itself, such a filibuster possesses no potency. Its only possible result can be to dramatize an issue and thus influence public opinion.

There is, however, another type of filibuster that aims to accomplish far more. That is the concerted effort of a sizable number of senators to prevent the transaction of any business until a bill they oppose is withdrawn or watered down. Knowing that the legislation will pass if it comes to a vote, they try to avoid such an eventuality by holding the floor indefinitely. The Senate is thus prevented from taking action on other bills unless it capitulates to them.

Some say that this collective version of the filibuster constitutes blackmail, pure and simple. In its most acute form, it may even put senators on notice that important national functions will have to halt for lack of funds unless the will of the minority is done. Yet the filibuster has its defenders. A disingenuous argument advanced by some of them is that senators should be courteous enough to hear out patiently any colleague who thinks he has something important to say. In reality, champions of the filibuster are motivated by a far more basic consideration.

THEORY AND PRACTICE

The theory behind the filibuster has been expounded effectively by the noted columnist, Walter Lippmann. When vital matters are involved, he argues, what is at stake may be of such

---

35 Experts are divided on the question of who delivered the longest Senate speech of all time. Those who would award the title to Strom Thurmond of South Carolina point out simply that no other senator has ever exceeded the record he established with a 24-hour speech against civil rights legislation in 1957. Partisans of Senator Morse, however, will not let it be forgotten that Thurmond's friends sustained him by requesting quorum calls every few hours so that he could leave the chamber briefly. Morse, on the other hand, demonstrated in his 23-hour speech against a tidelands oil bill that he had overcome the frailties that beset lesser men.

great moment that any legislation should have the backing of more than a simple majority in the Senate. Since controversial laws can be readily enforced only if "a very large majority" accepts them, significant minorities should have the opportunity to block solutions hostile to their vital interests. Lippmann believes that the filibuster is an effective means to this end, for it can be overcome only when an overwhelming majority insists on the legislation in question. Somewhat similarly, the conservative *New York Times* columnist Arthur Krock lays emphasis on the fact that "the Constitution established a republic, and not a mass-action democracy." And Professor Lindsay Rogers of Columbia University says flatly: "The filibuster is a weapon that the constitutional framers who constructed the Senate failed to anticipate but one that they would view with favor."

To a considerable extent, these opinions accord with the doctrine of the "concurrent majority," expounded by John C. Calhoun. The nineteenth-century American political theorist held that simple majority rule is logical only for a homogeneous population. In the more typical community, which consists of diverse interests, he felt that the counting of heads merely legalizes exploitation by the largest group. In a society consisting of four shoemakers and three tanners, for example, it would give rise to naked exploitation by the more numerous shoemakers. He recommended that each major interest group in a heterogeneous community should be given a defensive veto over actions affecting its fundamental concerns.

Calhoun, however, never dreamed of using his doctrine to justify giving a defensive veto to Negroes in order that they might protect themselves against the actions of whites. Quite to the contrary, he expounded his theory of the concurrent majority in such a way as to uphold the right of southern planters to exploit the Negro despite the disapprobation of the country as a whole.

Interestingly enough, the Senate filibuster in recent years has been utilized most often in behalf of a related cause: the obstruction of civil rights legislation. In view of the striking success that southerners had enjoyed with the filibuster in the past, they decided to use it again in 1960, after failing in their effort to keep civil rights from the floor.

Senator Johnson at once announced the method that he would employ to force an end to the filibuster: around-the-clock sessions of the Senate. The southerners would have to talk indefinitely for 24 hours a day if they were to keep the Senate from acting on civil rights. With the backing of Dirksen, the Majority Leader set February 29 as the date on which the ordeal would begin. He obtained the Senate's approval by a vote of 67 to 10.

Breaking the filibusterers physically, however, would be no easy task. With eighteen speakers available,[36] each southerner would have to hold the floor for an average of only eighty minutes a day to continue the filibuster indefinitely. To make even more efficient use of his forces, Senator Russell drew up a battle plan under which each of his men would be entitled to a three-day rest after speaking for only four hours. While one senator was orating, another would allow him to rest periodically by interpolating lengthy questions. As the two were "working a shift," the other southerners were to absent themselves from the Senate floor and even from the vicinity of the Capitol. Although they stayed away partly to rest, they had an even stronger motive. They hoped that their absence would help push attendance below 51, the quorum required to transact business. If that happened, the Senate would have to adjourn —just what every filibusterer yearns for. An adjournment is valuable because, when the Senate reconvenes, several time-consuming formalities must take place. Unless there is unanimous consent—and an objector is always available to block that—the journal of the preceding day must be read, for instance. Also, the "morning hour," in which senators introduce bills and insert items in the *Congressional Record,* eats up more time.

---

36 The senators from every southern state except Tennessee and Texas took part.

A TIME TO SPEAK

When the filibuster began, the fact that virtually none of the southerners would appear for quorum calls meant that almost all the senators supporting civil rights had to be available at any hour of the day or night. With southerners challenging the presence of a quorum at all hours, other members had to be instantly on call when the bells were rung. There was a wide choice of uncomfortable places in which to nap: army cots set up in various parts of the Capitol, office couches, and even the rubdown tables in the old Senate Office Building. Without a doubt the filibuster was exacting a far greater toll from the northerners than from their southern colleagues.[37]

IN 1964, THE SOUTHERN FILIBUSTER against civil rights took place in two distinct stages. In the first of these, the aim was to prevent the Senate from even voting to take up the House-passed bill. When this attempt failed, the second stage began: an effort to block a vote on the bill itself.

There was a procedural reason why twin filibusters were possible in 1964 while the southerners had to be content with a single marathon four years earlier. In 1960, the Democratic leadership had seized on a bill that was already on the floor—the one on Stella School Reorganization—and invited senators to tack on civil rights amendments. No vote was therefore necessary on a motion to call up civil rights, because technically the Senate was not considering that subject at all. But in 1964 no such tactic was available. The House had already passed a civil rights bill, and the question before the Senate concerned that bill.

The motion to take up the bill was to be made by the Majority Leader. Senator Mansfield badly wanted to

[37] Senator Case of New Jersey was so affected that he roused himself from a deep sleep and dashed into the Senate chamber to answer a quorum call that he had only dreamed about.

make his motion and have it voted on in the course of the "morning hour," a period reserved for such normally routine matters. For during the two hours that the "morning hour" lasts, there can be no debate on a motion of the type that he intended to offer. Thus the motion could be made and approved without any possibility of a filibuster.

But the southerners, who, of course, would gain from the dilatory debate that Mansfield hoped to prevent, planned to fritter away time so that the "morning hour" would be over before the Majority Leader could present his motion. They managed to kill almost half of the two hours just by insisting upon reading the previous day's Journal. Normally, this reading is dispensed with; but there must be unanimous consent for that to be done, and Senator Russell quickly interposed an objection. The reading of the Journal—the official record of actions taken, and of communications received from the President and from the House—consumed 44 minutes. Then Russell earned the right to speak for the remainder of the time by moving that the Journal be amended to include additional matter. That motion was debatable, and of course its author chose to discuss it at great length. By the time he yielded the floor, the "morning hour" was over and Senator Mansfield had no alternative but to make his motion in a parliamentary context permitting full debate. As had been expected, the first stage of the filibuster began at once.

The filibusterers were well organized. Their team was divided into three platoons, so that no individual would be subjected to very much physical strain. While the members of one platoon held the floor, the others could do what they chose and be where they chose. They usually chose, of course, not to be on the Senate floor.

Senators supporting civil rights could enjoy no such leisurely pace. At all times, enough of *them* had to be on the floor, or at least within reach, so that a quorum of 51 members could be produced whenever the southerners demanded one. The absence of a quorum at this preliminary stage could be almost disastrous because of a peculiarity in the rules. On a motion to take up a bill, each senator may deliver no more than two speeches in the course of any single legislative day. But unlike a *calendar* day, a *legislative* day lasts until there is a formal adjournment of the Senate. During the civil rights struggle, it was therefore in the interest of the southerners for the Senate to adjourn, rather than recess, every day or so in order that each filibusterer would again have the right to deliver two lengthy speeches. Since an adjournment is automatic when a quorum cannot be produced, the proponents of civil rights had to be readily available to avoid playing the southerners' game.

They were readily available, however, and the hopes of the southerners faded. Consequently, it finally became possible—two weeks after Senator Mansfield had first made his motion—to set a time for voting on whether to take up the bill. When the vote came, the Mansfield motion was carried, with 67 senators registering their approval, and only 17—all southerners—casting negative votes. Stage 1 of the filibuster was over.

Without further ado, the second stage began. Now the substantive issue of civil rights, not the procedural issue of whether to consider a bill, was before the Senate.

During filibusters which had taken place in previous years, civil rights senators had generally abandoned the floor to the southerners in the belief that they would talk themselves out more quickly if not allowed to rest their vocal cords while northern members were giving speeches. But this time a different strategy was adopted. The friends of the bill would not only participate in the debate but would actually take the lead in carrying it on. In this way the attention of the press would not be riveted exclusively on what the southerners were saying;

the arguments on the other side, too, would be presented. Moreover, after a few weeks of such give-and-take, all senators would have to concede that the bill had received careful study. Since many members had not yet committed themselves on the legislation, this procedure might influence the decision whether or not to end the debate and begin voting.

It was Senator Humphrey who began presenting the detailed case for the bill. In addition to serving as lead-off speaker, the Minnesota senator also took over the functions of floor manager. This assignment normally goes to the chairman of the committee or subcommittee which has reported a bill. The civil rights legislation, however, had not been reported by any committee, and in those circumstances it was natural for President Johnson and Senator Mansfield to look to Mr. Humphrey. Long before assuming the title of Majority Whip (entailing responsibilities as Deputy Majority Leader), Humphrey had earned a reputation as one of the most passionate advocates of civil rights in the Senate. Since, in addition, he was a most skillful legislative technician, it was logical to put him in charge of the bill and allow him to make the crucial tactical decisions.

The most important strategic decision, however, had already been made: the bill would not be handled as a partisan Democratic project. Accordingly, Humphrey invited the Republican Whip, Thomas H. Kuchel of California, to work with him in steering the bill to final passage. The two men then assigned each section of the legislation to a pair of senators—one a Democrat and the other a Republican—for detailed analysis on the floor and for managing during the amendment stage. Never before had the liberals been organized this well.

Their coordination even extended to the preparation of a bipartisan civil rights newsletter, which briefed the friends of the bill each day on how the arguments of the southerners could be answered. The newsletter also nagged, wheedled, and cajoled the civil rights senators to be on the floor whenever they were needed. An elaborate bipartisan alerting system, featuring an impressively efficient telephone network, kept morale high by making it possible to round up quorums in record time while still allowing rotating groups of members to remain away from the floor at periodic intervals.

The quorums were produced, the arguments of the southerners were answered, and the affirmative case for the legislation was made. When a southerner took the floor, he could seldom count on completing his prepared speech without interruption. In completely unprecedented fashion, senators who supported civil rights were there to pepper him with disconcerting questions and even, occasionally, extract significant concessions. Senator Allen J. Ellender (D., La.), for example, was maneuvered into an admission that some southern Negroes were indeed kept from voting because of their race. It was not an earth-shaking revelation but it carried weight because it came from a southern senator.

What Humphrey and Kuchel wanted, however, was not to score debating points but rather to get an agreement that voting could begin. On this, however, the southerners were adamant. For six long weeks, they refused to allow even a single amendment to be acted on. Certainly they had no intention of permitting a vote on the bill itself.

Unlike Lyndon Johnson in 1960, Senator Mansfield did not try to make the southerners surrender by scheduling all-night sessions. The Majority Leader was a gentle man, and he was worried about the effect that 'round-the-clock debate might have on the health of his elderly colleagues. Besides, Johnson's policy had by no means produced significant results during the filibuster four years earlier.

As the days wore on during the 1960 filibuster, liberals became increasingly impatient with Johnson's approach. They felt that the Majority Leader was not taking advantage of the only reasonably effective weapon against filibusters—the imposition of cloture.

LIMITATION OF DEBATE

Cloture is a method that Rule XXII of the Senate sanctions for cutting off debate. Until 1917, there was no such provision. In that year, antiwar senators waged a successful filibuster against Woodrow Wilson's bill to arm American merchant ships against German submarines. The President poured fire and brimstone on those who had defeated him. "A little group of willful men, representing no opinion but their own, have rendered the great government of the United States helpless and contemptible," he raged. The Chief Executive broadened his attack to encompass the Senate rules that had made his defeat possible. "The Senate of the United States," he said, "is the only legislative body in the world which cannot act when its majority is ready for action." Yielding to the pressure generated by Wilson's denunciation, the Senate adopted the first cloture rule in its history.

The new Rule XXII provided that the cloture procedure could be initiated by a petition bearing the signatures of sixteen senators. Two days after the petition was filed, the Senate would vote on whether to impose a limitation on debate. The approval of two-thirds of those present and voting would be required. In the event that this unlikely majority could be put together, each senator could still have the floor for one additional hour.

In the first ten years of its life, cloture was successfully invoked only four times. If the rule was not exactly overworked between 1917 and 1927, it positively atrophied after that decade. The astonishing fact was that, as of 1960, cloture had never again been voted.

Almost half of the nineteen unsuccessful attempts to impose cloture had involved civil rights bills. On four of those occasions, a majority of the Senate favored cloture, but the two-thirds requirement could not be met. In each instance, opponents of the particular legislation, joined by the senators who opposed cloture as a matter of principle, were enough to make up the necessary one-third-plus-one.

Through the years preceding the Eighty-sixth Congress, every attempt to liberalize the cloture rule had failed. In fact, the Senate decided in 1949 to make it somewhat harder to limit debate. During a parliamentary battle preceding consideration of civil rights legislation, it stiffened Rule XXII to provide that two-thirds of the entire Senate membership would have to agree if cloture was to be imposed; approval by two-thirds of those present and voting would no longer suffice.

COMPROMISE OF 1959

On the opening day of the Eighty-sixth Congress, liberals had been up in arms about how difficult it still was to obtain cloture. As they had done in several other Congresses, they demanded a major overhaul of Rule XXII. The two-thirds requirement, they said, should be trimmed to a simple majority. Failing this, they would certainly be willing to settle for nothing less than a three-fifths rule. Within a few days, however, they had suffered an inglorious defeat. The architect of their humiliation was the Democratic leader.

Johnson took the initiative in the debate by offering a cloture resolution of his own. It represented, he said, a middle-of-the-road approach that avoided the extreme positions of the northern liberals, who demanded majority cloture, and the southern intransigents, who opposed any change whatever in the rule. The Majority Leader's proposal called for a return to the pre-1949 formula, permitting two-thirds of those present and voting to impose cloture.

Liberals were quick to charge that the "compromise" Johnson was promoting would make little difference in the existing situation. On a question as controversial as imposing cloture, few if any senators would be inclined to absent themselves. Thus, "two-thirds of those voting" and "two-thirds of the entire membership" might well turn out to be the same thing. In any event, the liberals noted, the arrangement Johnson now wanted to revive had proved almost totally useless during the period when it was in effect, from 1917 to 1949.

The Majority Leader had no patience with the critics of his resolution. When Douglas asked him to offer "a rather full explanation" of his compromise instead of "pushing for a very quick vote," he retorted that such a speech "would be criticized as being a southern filibuster." Since he did not know "how long it takes to explain a thing" to Douglas, he would be willing to write out his proposal, "if the senator can see better than he can hear."

Supported by Dirksen, Johnson had the votes to win. The first proof of this came when Clinton P. Anderson of New Mexico asked the Senate to agree that at the opening of a new Congress, Rule XXII—or any other rule—could be changed by a simple majority vote. On Johnson's motion, that proposal was tabled, 60–36. In like fashion, Douglas' plea for majority cloture was rejected, 67–28, and a three-fifths compromise offered by Senator Thruston B. Morton of Kentucky failed, 58–36. When all the alternatives were out of the way, Johnson's new two-thirds rule was put to a roll call vote. It won easy approval, 72–22.

Some liberals felt that they had been struck a foul blow. As they saw it, the Majority Leader had recognized that there was enough pressure to make some change in the cloture rule inevitable, but had contrived to satisfy the demand for action with the mere appearance of change.[38]

It was under the new Johnson rule that the Senate functioned during the Eighty-sixth Congress. To impose cloture, an almost impossible two-thirds vote would be needed. A bipartisan group of civil rights senators, however, decided to make the effort, since

---

[38] They were not consoled by the fact that under another section of the compromise it would now for the first time be possible for two-thirds of those present and voting to limit debate on a motion to change the rules (to make cloture easier, for example). This advantage, they felt, was completely canceled out by another element of the compromise: a provision establishing the doctrine that Senate rules (including, of course, Rule XXII) carry over automatically from one Congress to the next.

it appeared that continuous sessions were accomplishing nothing against the filibuster.

Before the petition they were circulating could be presented, Senator Morse filed one on his own. His document contained only one signature—that of Wayne Morse. As a consequence, it had no official status, since the rules require sixteen names. When, without explanation, Morse placed it on the clerk's desk anyway, Senator Morton of Kentucky, who was also chairman of the Republican National Committee, could not contain himself. In a fury, he marched to the desk, picked up the discharge petition, and tore it into hundreds of tiny pieces, which he proceeded to scatter over the carpet. Morse later interpreted this behavior for his fellow senators. Morton had subsequently explained to him, he said, that if a cloture petition was to be filed, it would be a Republican who would do the filing. The Democrat was tolerant. "I can well understand," he said, "how the chairman of the National Republican Party might want to have a cloture petition in this debate filed from the Republican side of the aisle. . . . None of us would have to be hit on the head with a baseball bat to know. . . ."

Morton held his peace when the bipartisan group filed *its* cloture petition. The petition contained almost twice the number of names needed. For cloture to be adopted, however, the thirty-one senators who had signed would have to win the support of approximately an equal number of their colleagues.

It was evident at once that they would get no help from the leadership. Johnson stated bluntly: "I hope the members of the Senate who desire legislation passed at this session of the Congress dealing with the subject of human rights will not support a motion to close debate, because I do not think that will be in the interest of passing any legislation. It will be only in the interest of perpetuating an issue." He argued that the petition was premature, for only after several items had been stripped from the Senate's civil rights bill would there be a chance to obtain the two-thirds support necessary to limit debate. There first had to be almost universal agreement, he said, about the principal ingredients that a civil rights bill should contain. Too many

PETITION FOR CLOTURE

We, the undersigned Senators, in accordance with the provisions of Rule XXII of the Standing Rules of the Senate, hereby move to bring to a close the debate upon the amendment (In the nature of a substitute) proposed by Mr. DIRKSEN to the bill (H. R. 8315) to authorize the Secretary of the Army to lease a portion of Fort Crowder, Missouri, to Stella Reorganized Schools R-1, Missouri.

Cloture petition to terminate Senate debate in 1960. Petition, requiring 16 names, attracted 31, but cloture was defeated on floor.

senators would refuse to back cloture as long as there was a possibility that provisions objectionable to them might be included in the final bill. The leader of the minority said that he, too, "could not sign the petition at the present time." Before acting, Dirksen recommended, the Senate should see what kind of bill the House would pass.

CLOTURE VOTE

Although the galleries were packed when the cloture motion came to a vote, there was no real suspense. The attitude of the leadership had doomed the attempt. Not only did the motion fail to command the support of the necessary two-thirds; it could not even win a simple majority of those present. The vote was 53–42. On neither side of the aisle had cloture been backed. The Democrats had opposed it, 33–30; the Republicans, 20–12. Fighters for a strong civil rights bill had suffered a disaster. Their plight was especially desperate because Johnson had called off the day-and-night sessions when the cloture petition was filed. After the vain nine-day effort to wear the filibusterers down physically, not even *that* weapon was now available. Never had the civil rights cause seemed more hopeless.

AS THEY HAD DONE in 1960, civil rights supporters resorted to an attempt at cloture in 1964. But this time their morale was high. Four years earlier, they had felt merely a sense of going through the motions, with no real hope of success. Now victory seemed possible and perhaps even likely. Senator Russell's "no compromise" policy—encouraged by the strong showing of Governor Wallace of Alabama in several of the Democratic primaries—had alienated many who were on the fence, for only a few diehards still thought that the Negro revolution could be contained in the absence of major legislative concessions. In addition, President Johnson could be counted on for some help in the effort to round up support for cloture.

Without the cooperation of the Republicans, however, the fight might still be lost. Everything seemed to depend on the part that one particular Republican would choose to play as the showdown approached. The key man was Everett McKinley Dirksen, Minority Leader of the Senate.

From the very start, Dirksen held his cards close to his vest. A civil rights bill was desirable, he would say, but the Senate should not allow itself to be used as a rubber stamp. Serious defects were to be found in the House bill, he maintained. For one thing, the public accommodations section was too broad. For another, the section on equal employment needed overhauling. A number of drastic changes would have to be made. As many as seventy amendments might be necessary.

But having thus established his credentials as an independent-minded critic of the House bill, Dirksen chose to play a peculiar role. With senators who were not committed on the bill looking to him for guidance, he led them gradually and even imperceptibly into the civil rights camp. The man who had insisted on seventy amendments soon let it be known that this was merely his asking price. In no time at all, he had pared down his demands so drastically that only a few major differences remained between the bill he wanted and the one that had been passed by the House.

To help bridge the gap that still did exist, extensive negotiations were initiated. Taking part in them were Attorney General Kennedy and other high officials of the Justice Department as well as senators from both parties, including Dirksen and Humphrey. The House bill was subjected to the kind of minute analysis that usually takes place in committee. Although Dirksen backed and filled and hemmed and hawed, he decided eventually to go along, and agreement was reached on a bipartisan package that everyone promised to support.

The package did contain several provisions that weakened the House bill. For example, the Attorney General would not in every case be able to file suits on his own to end discrimination in public accommodations or employment; unless there was a pattern or practice of such discrimination, he would have to wait for a private individual to go to court before he could intervene. Moreover, in a state which had its own antidiscrimination agency, there could be no federal enforcement of the law until that agency had been given a chance to act on complaints. And when federal funds were withheld from a state program in which discrimination was practiced, the withholding of funds would not apply beyond the offending county or municipality. Apart from these changes, however, the provisions of the strong House bill were left virtually untouched. The legislation would still be the most potent on civil rights in almost a century. And now that the doubts of the most reluctant dragon of them all had been resolved, other senators who had been hesitating would probably decide to go along, too.

Why had Dirksen elected to use his power in such Byzantine fashion to improve the chances that civil rights would carry the day? His own explanation, which he offered to the Senate, was a reference to what Victor Hugo is supposed to have said on the night that he died: "Stronger than all the armies is an idea whose time has come." The senator, who was receiving ten letters against the bill for every one in favor, explained that civil rights was an idea whose time had come and it was pointless to try to stop the march of history. The cynics scoffed. They said that Dirksen had made a deal with the Administration and would be well rewarded for his cooperation on civil rights. But at least one other factor was involved. Dirksen, like Johnson, knew that there was likely to be bloodshed if a far-reaching bill was not passed, and he wanted neither his party nor its leader in the Senate to be open to the charge that a call to statesmanship had gone unanswered.

Whatever the motive, the importance of Dirksen's actions could not be overstated. As *The New York Times* described it: "What Dirksen did was to piece together a substitute for the House-passed bill so near the original that it was acceptable to the Justice Department and the bipartisan civil rights coalition, and sufficiently different in tone and emphasis to win the few crucial Republican votes needed for cloture." Senator Mansfield said simply: "This is his finest hour."

Certainly the "Mansfield-Dirksen substitute," as it came to be called, represented enormous progress. Yet there was still no certainty that the compromise commanded the support of the two-thirds majority needed to impose cloture. No stone was left unturned in the quest for additional votes. When a number of Republican senators indicated that they might balk at cloture unless the Senate was permitted to decide whether to incorporate certain amendments they were sponsoring in the bipartisan package, the leadership decided not to stand in the way. In the voting that followed, one of the proposed amendments—to allow a trial by jury in certain contempt cases arising under the Act—was approved and the other two were rejected. The important thing, however, was that the senators who had promoted the amendment felt that their rights had been protected and that they could now vote to end the debate. Cloture seemed more likely than ever.

The actual petition for cloture, signed by a bipartisan group of 39 members, was filed by Senators Mansfield and Dirksen on June 8th. Two days later the galleries were packed for the cloture vote. In a dramatic final hour of debate, the principals in the protracted battle made their appeals. There were speeches by Mansfield and Humphrey, and also one by Dirksen. And there was an address by Senator Russell, whose Senate would never again be the same if cloture was imposed on a civil rights bill.

Russell, however, would have to adjust to the new reality. With all 100 members of the Senate present to take part in the proceedings, 67 votes would be needed to bring the debate to an end. There were more than enough. When the roll call was completed, 71 senators—44 Democrats and 27 Republicans—had voted to impose cloture. On the other side were only 23 Democrats (almost all of them southerners) and 6 Republicans. The latter group included Barry Goldwater, who later the same year would make opposition to federal protection of civil rights an important part of his campaign for the presidency.

Although the proponents of cloture had anticipated—correctly, as it turned out—that they would have votes to spare, they had taken no chances, even arranging for the participation of a member literally at death's door. Senator Clair Engle (D., Calif.), who had just undergone a brain operation, was brought to the floor in a wheelchair. His speech failed him, but the senator managed to motion feebly with his hand that he wished to be recorded for cloture.

If still another vote was needed, it, too, was available. It was arranged that Senator Hayden of Arizona should remain in the cloakroom when the names of all the senators were called for the first time. Had the roll call revealed that cloture could not pass without his support, he would have saved the day by voting "aye." As it was, the battle was won without him, so Hayden could vote as he had always done: against any attack on the filibuster, dearly prized by senators from small states as a device to prevent them from being overwhelmed by the sheer weight of numbers.

President Johnson applauded the Senate for its approval of cloture. "Today's action," he said, "demonstrates that the national will manifests itself in congressional action." He did not mention that it had taken 74 long days for the manifestation to appear.

Fate of Senate Amendments

AFTER THE DEFEAT of cloture in 1960, the filibuster went on, and southern senators continued to fill the air with denunciations of the Supreme Court and all its works. When Dirksen asked unanimous consent for a civil rights opinion by the court to be printed in the *Congressional Record,* Eastland objected, "I do not want this Record cluttered by such crap as the court writes." Eventually he relented—not because he had changed his mind about the court, but rather because he had remembered that, in his words, "*much* crap is printed in the Record." In both instances, he later must have had second thoughts about his use of the four-letter word, for he took advantage of his right to revise the remarks before they were printed in the *Congressional Record.* In the first quotation he changed the word to "claptrap"; in the second, it became "useless material." [39]

Listening to such denunciations of the Supreme Court was by no means the greatest provocation that the liberals had to endure. Far more galling was the tactic that the leadership was using to carve out a bill that would be "acceptable" to the Senate.

The method was as maddening as it was deadly. Each time a strengthening amendment was offered, a motion to table it would be made. Since such a motion may not be debated, no filibuster could prevent it from being voted upon. But for once the southerners could remain undisturbed at the prospect of losing their most effective weapon. They were, in fact, in the enviable position of standing to gain a great deal from the vote

[39] The right of congressmen to edit their floor statements before publication in the *Congressional Record* has frequently come under sharp criticism. The late Senator Richard L. Neuberger of Oregon said that a legislator "is evidently the only person on earth who can sigh, 'I wish I'd said that,' and then actually say it!" He wrote of having observed senators busily engaged in expunging comments or "adding afterthoughts which may furnish an extra fillip to a reply that was flat or uneffective when uttered."

while risking absolutely nothing. For, although approval of the tabling motion would kill outright the amendment they opposed, defeat of the motion would not mean that the amendment had been adopted. There would still have to be an affirmative effort to add it to the bill. And if that attempt was made, the southerners would, as usual, have the right to filibuster.

Implementation of the strategy, once it began to operate, rested for the most part with those who had devised it. Often it was Johnson himself, or Dirksen, who offered the motion to table; at other times the motion was made by a member who was close to the leadership. The senator who planned to make the tabling motion would obtain the floor and announce that before introducing it formally he would yield some time to speakers who wanted to be heard on the amendment. It was of course understood that at his pleasure he could cut off such speeches and force a vote. In a sense, this was a specialized form of cloture, available only for the purpose of defeating legislation. The parceling out of time was actually forcing the Senate to operate under the kind of rigid debate limitation usually associated with the House.[40] Yet senators who at other times derided the House for restricting debate by means of "gag rules" were singularly acquiescent in the leadership's tactic.

Johnson and Dirksen knew, of course, that the Senate always has the right to reconsider a tabling action—once. They followed the usual custom, however, and prevented this from occurring in any meaningful sense by moving *immediate* reconsideration, and then getting the Senate to table *that* motion. Over and again, the *Congressional Record* would report a reasonable facsimile of the following:

MR. JOHNSON of Texas. Mr. President, I move that the vote by which the amendments were laid on the table be reconsidered.

---

40 Except through use of the tabling device, the Senate can impose a limitation on debate only when unanimous consent is obtained (or, of course, when cloture is invoked). Generally, the majority leader makes a unanimous consent request only after first conferring with the minority leader on a satisfactory timetable for the consideration of a bill.

MR. DIRKSEN. Mr. President, I move to lay on the table the motion to reconsider.

THE PRESIDING OFFICER. The question is on agreeing to the motion to lay on the table the motion to reconsider.

The motion to lay on the table was agreed to.

Sometimes the roles were reversed, but always the lethal effect was the same: later reconsideration was foreclosed.

A considerable number of southern amendments, too, were killed in this way. But on balance the use of the tabling practice was highly disadvantageous to the civil rights senators. Since they could produce a strong bill only by means of floor amendments, every successful tabling motion directed against one of their proposals hit at the very core of their strategy. The position of the southerners was very different. Although the crippling amendments they offered might be shelved, their grand design was unaffected. The filibuster, or the threat of using it, was still available to them.

THE PARLIAMENTARY CONTEXT in which the Senate voted on amendments four years later could not have been more different than in 1960. At that time, with cloture having been rejected, there could be no voting except on tabling motions, and that kind of voting could only result in the defeat of northern motions designed to strengthen an otherwise weak bill. Now, in sharp contrast, the Senate was operating under cloture, and the bill that it was considering had sharp teeth already. Thus it was the southerners, not the civil rights senators, who now had an interest in offering amendments. And offer amendments they did, in almost embarrassing profusion. Altogether, 107 proposed changes were called up and voted on. But the shower of votes accomplished almost nothing; no substantial alterations were made in the bill.

Southern senators complained bitterly that there was insufficient time to explain their amendments adequately. It was understandable that they found it disconcerting to switch from debating-without-voting to voting-without-debating. Life under cloture meant that each senator had only a single hour in which to speak both on the proposed amendments to the bill and on the bill itself. The time could be consumed all at once, in a single 60-minute oration, or the member could split his hour into any number of segments he desired. Some southerners, in order to participate in more than one portion of the debate, practiced segmentation to a point that approached absurdity, yielding themselves as little as 30 seconds at a time. Unaccustomed as they were to public speaking of this sort, they became increasingly fretful, particularly when they saw that every amendment they really cared about was going to be defeated ignominiously. Striking back in the only way they could, they demanded time-consuming roll-call votes on nearly every amendment instead of allowing voice votes. On a single day, the roll had to be called 34 times, thus setting a new record. The leadership chafed, but there was consolation in the knowledge that eventually the southerners would run out of amendments: the only amendments in order were those that had been offered before cloture was imposed. The moment was thus approaching for the voting that really counted.

ACCENT ON VOTING

As Senate debate proceeded in 1960, time seemed to be running out for those who wanted a strong bill. The civil rights senators were particularly alarmed when the leadership began saying that an omnibus civil rights statute was not even really needed. If some progress could merely be made toward Negro voting, Johnson and Dirksen argued, that would be enough, for winning the ballot would enable the Negro to protect effectively all his other rights.

The suggestion that the vote alone could emancipate the Negro was not new. Attorney General Rogers had once put it this way:

> The right to vote . . . occupies a key position because it provides a means of protecting other rights. When minority groups exercise their franchise more effectively, it almost invariably follows that they achieve a greater measure of other fundamental freedoms.

Those who shared this point of view noted the substantial results achieved by Negro political power in the North. For example, the New York City Council had been persuaded to ban discrimination in housing; some states had been led to adopt fair employment practice laws; and wherever the Negro could vote, there was less discrimination in public places.

Yet, in an important sense, the situation is markedly different in the South. There, even when the Negro has succeeded in defeating all the elaborate attempts that have been made to prevent him from voting,[41] he has often won only the dubious privilege of choosing between two white supremacists. At least up to now, his vote has become a serious factor only in southern municipal elections.

Those senators afflicted by doubts like these were, however, being increasingly stigmatized in the Eighty-sixth Congress as malcontents who refused to recognize that a little progress was better than none. Sentiment was steadily crystallizing in favor of a "moderate" bill. Senators Johnson and Dirksen were working hand-in-glove to make this tendency prevail.

A QUESTION OF DEGREE

The unusually close cooperation between Johnson and Dirksen was patent at virtually every stage of the civil rights struggle in 1960. A good working arrangement between opposing leaders

---

41 Sometimes these attempts were direct and even blatant, like "white primary" laws and literacy tests that only Negroes were obliged to take. When such overt discrimination was struck down by the courts, and when devices like the poll tax no longer seemed to deter Negroes, economic pressure and physical intimidation would make their appearance. And always one could count on cooperative state officials who would simply refuse to register Negroes, or apply voting requirements such as literacy tests so unfairly that Negro teachers with advanced college degrees were failed while barely literate whites experienced no difficulty. (The Civil Rights Commission publicized the case of one Negro in Louisiana whose registration had been successfully challenged because of what the registrar called his "error in spilling.")

is undeniably desirable, for without it the Senate would often be unable to conduct its affairs efficiently. If, for example, the Minority Leader were not consulted regarding the scheduling of legislation for floor debate, he could retaliate by withholding the unanimous consent that the Majority Leader needs to transact much of the Senate's business. Nevertheless, the sweetness and light that characterized the relationship between Johnson and Dirksen went far beyond the demands of practical etiquette. It was, as a matter of fact, something noteworthy in the annals of the Senate. In the past, rival Senate leaders had at least sometimes conformed to this description by Floyd M. Riddick, the Senate parliamentarian:

> [They] appear to the visitor in the galleries to be generals of enemy camps. During heated debates on certain partisan issues or particular conflicts on procedure, one can observe the flushed faces of the two leaders as they stand across the aisle from each other and shake their fists and make emphatic assertions. Their actions on some occasions are so pugnacious that a visitor would assume that they had really never spoken to each other privately. . . .[42]

In sharp contrast, Johnson and Dirksen were a study in togetherness.

The alliance between the two leaders made Johnson's power almost absolute. It meant that on occasions when the liberals deserted his leadership, he could compensate for their defection with votes that Dirksen controlled. Even when Dirksen was not his ally, Johnson could exercise a vast amount of authority. As floor leader, he also headed the Democratic Policy Committee, which schedules legislation for floor debate, and its Steering Committee, which gives majority senators their committee assignments. He completely dominated the party conference, or caucus, which is nominally the supreme party organ in the Senate. (In fact, through most of his reign, the caucus met only infrequently, and then simply to reelect the majority leader and other party officers and to hear Johnson deliver a miniature State of the Union address outlining the course he would

---

42 *The U.S. Congress: Organization and Procedure* (Washington: National Capitol Publishers, Inc., 1949), 100.

like the Senate to pursue.) Johnson's power, however, derived not merely from the offices he held but from the toughness and adroitness with which he handled wavering senators—on the floor, in the cloakroom, and wherever else they were to be found.

With the assistance of Dirksen, Johnson spread the word that the Senate leadership favored a bill devoted almost exclusively to voting. He had reason to believe that this was precisely the sort of bill that would eventually emerge from the House. His tactic, therefore, was to persuade the Senate that it should postpone any action of its own in anticipation of the House bill. Obediently, the Senate began to tread water, awaiting a signal from the House as to the course it should follow.

Discharge Petition in the House

ATTENTION in the House still centered on Representative Celler's petition to discharge the Rules Committee of responsibility for the civil rights bill. With the reconvening of Congress in January 1960, liberals launched a massive campaign to add signatures to the petition.

Shortly after the new session began, the document had an impressive total of 175 names. Although the figure was tantalizingly close to the required number (219), it was still too far away to constitute effective pressure on the Rules Committee. In an attempt to remedy that situation, national organizations interested in civil rights conducted an elaborate lobbying operation at the Capitol. As they spoke to leaders of the House, they emphasized their conviction that only the discharge petition could free the bill from the Rules Committee. Among the lobbyists were the legislative director of the American Federation of Labor-Congress of Industrial Organizations, the president of the United Automobile Workers, the executive secretary of the NAACP, and the president of the American

Jewish Congress. It was an imposing array. But its efforts failed to inspire any mass signing of the discharge petition.

Two weeks later, a newly formed organization of House liberals—the Democratic Study Group [43]—employed what it hoped would be an effective technique to dramatize the issue: a full day of pro-civil rights speeches in the House. No important legislative business was transacted on January 27, as speaker after speaker, each of whom had previously obtained a "special order" [44] to address the House, discussed civil rights and, in particular, the discharge petition. Many referred bitingly to efforts allegedly being made by Minority Leader Halleck to dissuade Republicans from signing. His motive, they charged, was to maintain the conservative alliance with the South.[45] Not many reporters, however, even heard the charges, for there is nothing like extended oratory to empty a Congressional Press Gallery. Only the reader who was highly discriminating in selecting a daily newspaper even knew that the speeches had been delivered, not to mention what they contained.

NEW PRESSURE APPLIED

Although the Study Group failed in its forensic effort, the next attempt it made to win support for the discharge petition was more productive. Leaders of the liberal bloc felt there was many a representative who would face irresistible pressure from his constituents if only they could be informed that he had not yet signed the petition. But according to House practice, the names on a discharge petition are not revealed unless and until the necessary majority is obtained. The Study Group deter-

---

43 Leaders of the Study Group were Lee Metcalf (now a senator from Montana) and Frank Thompson, Jr. of New Jersey. Stewart Udall, now Secretary of the Interior, was a prominent member.

44 A "special order" is an authorization to dispense with the regular rules of procedure in order to make it possible for a representative to speak or for a particular item of business to be considered. The issuance of a special order requires unanimous consent or the approval of the Rules Committee.

45 The Minority Leader was always nettled by such comments. He did not appreciate having his "motives impugned by talk about an unholy alliance." Democrats, he charged, were converting the civil rights struggle into "a political operation to make us the goats."

mined that the nonsigners had to be identified even though this would involve the disclosure of confidential information. To accomplish their end, they decided on something of a ruse.

While signatures are being solicited, a discharge petition remains on the Speaker's desk. There, a congressman may have access to it for the purpose of signing it or withdrawing his signature—or refreshing his memory as to whether he has already signed. What the leaders of the organization proposed was very simple. Each member was made responsible for a group of names. He would stroll up to the Speaker's desk and pretend to be studying the petition—while actually checking to see whether it contained any of the names he had been assigned to track down. In this way it would be possible to compile an accurate list of the members who had signed the document.

The Study Group enthusiastically approved the strategy. During the next few days, there seemed to be an epidemic of forgetfulness among liberal Democrats as to whether they had already subscribed to the petition. There was much "nonchalant" perusal of the restricted document and, in due course, the complete list of signatories was turned over to a grateful *New York Times,* which at once proceeded to publish it.

Democratic leaders of the House, who usually insisted on meticulous observance of the rules, looked the other way this time. Of the 175 names on the list, 145 belonged to Democrats. There was no embarrassment for that party. But the situation of the Republicans was quite different. The country now knew that only thirty of *them* had signed. It was dangerous, in a presidential election year, to be stigmatized as the party obstructing civil rights.

Minority Leader Halleck was incensed at the leak. It not only exposed the negative Republican position, but would almost certainly add many more signatures to the petition. Halleck, however, was helpless. The damage had already been done. The names were in the public domain, and a flock of belated converts were finding their way to the Speaker's desk.

Use of the discharge petition struck some congressmen as procedurally unorthodox. But they were reassured by the attitude of Speaker Rayburn, a stickler for observance of the rules. Although he himself abstained from signing, he made it clear that only custom was holding him back. He said significantly: "The way to get [the civil rights bill] up is to sign a petition." There was no question that the Speaker was throwing his considerable weight on the side of discharge.

It was under this almost irresistible combination of pressures that Chairman Smith of the Rules Committee finally surrendered. With the petition only 29 signatures short of the required number, he announced that within a week his committee would hold hearings on H.R. 8601. The action, he said alliteratively, would be taken without "dilly, delay, or dally." If the bill had been held up unnecessarily, he insisted, the blame should be laid at the door of Congressman Celler, who had imprisoned it in his Judiciary Committee for the first seven months of 1959. Celler, he suggested, had been interested in making political hay, not in passing a civil rights bill.

Smith was not the first to make the charge that Celler and other northern Democrats desired first and foremost to gain political advantage from the civil rights controversy. Throughout the struggle, Republicans had maintained that Celler would have used different tactics had he really been concerned about civil rights. According to this argument, he concentrated public attention on the discharge petition only to embarrass the many Republicans who would not sign. Although he knew that they opposed the device on principle, he could easily accuse them of maliciously blocking the only available road to civil rights.

ALTERNATIVE ROUTES

The indictment of Celler was predicated on the theory that a civil rights bill could have been brought to the floor without a discharge petition. There were, in fact, two other possible methods. The one most discussed was a procedure that is known as Calendar Wednesday.

House rules set aside one day each week on which committees may bring directly to the floor measures they do not want to channel through the Rules Committee. The Majority Leader normally secures unanimous consent in advance that Calendar Wednesday be dispensed with for the week. Although his request is almost always granted, the need for unanimity still means that any member can object and force the House to follow the regular order. Why had Celler not interposed such an objection?

In a speech to the House, the Judiciary Committee chairman declared that such a step would have been singularly unhelpful to the civil rights bill. Because of a chance circumstance, he explained, reliance on Calendar Wednesday would have killed the possibility of early House action on civil rights. The rule provides that on Wednesday committees are invited *in alphabetical order* to present bills for floor consideration. The Judiciary Committee ranked twelfth in the listing, and each committee ahead of it could occupy an entire day. Thus eleven Wednesdays might pass before the House had exhausted the letters from "A" to "I" ("Agriculture" to "Interstate and Foreign Commerce"), and "Judiciary" would finally get its turn. Celler suspected that few chairmen would forego the opportunity to bring up bills when their committees were called, for seven of the eleven committees with alphabetical priority over Judiciary were chaired by congressmen openly opposed to civil rights. Because of these factors as well as other opportunities for delay that would be available, he feared that civil rights could be postponed by parliamentary maneuvering until the closing days of the session. And a rule stipulates that there can be no Calendar Wednesday during the last two weeks before adjournment.

The historical record on which Celler could rely was impressive. Calendar Wednesday had last been used successfully a full ten years earlier, when it had freed from the grip of the Rules Committee a bill that later became the Fair Employment Practices Act. That feat had been accomplished only after the House had endured elaborate time-wasting procedures—and the name of the committee involved in the FEPC fight

(Banking and Currency) had a far more favorable alphabetical status than the Judiciary Committee.[46]

There was one other procedure by which the Rules Committee might have been bypassed. On two Mondays each month, a motion to "suspend the rules" would have been in order. This meant that Celler could have brought H.R. 8601 to an immediate vote, although passage of the bill through this procedure would have required approval by two-thirds instead of by a simple majority. Considering events in retrospect, it is likely that this approval could have been obtained, since the bill was eventually supported almost three-to-one. Why, then, did Cellar not use the suspension method?

The explanation offered by the New York congressman was that the procedure would have been inadequate, for if it was used the committee bill would not have been open to floor amendment. Celler's consistent position had been that the meager measure recommended by his committee possessed great value in that it would enable liberals to attach significant amendments. With the wisdom of hindsight, it is now clear that nothing would have been lost through recourse to the suspension procedure, for there simply were not enough liberal votes to strengthen the bill on the floor. The Judiciary Committee chairman, a veteran of almost forty years in the House, may have been canny enough to suspect in advance that this would be the case and to have chosen the discharge procedure only as a means of exposing Republican hypocrisy on the subject of civil rights.

Whatever the reason, Celler rejected both Calendar Wednesday and suspension of the rules in favor of the discharge petition, and this strategy did succeed in prying the bill out of the Rules Committee. That the tactic had indeed been successful was indicated when the Rules Committee announced

---

[46] Only one month after the civil rights vote in the House, Calendar Wednesday was again successfully employed, to save a bill providing federal assistance to economically depressed areas. As in 1950, the committee involved was Banking and Currency.

that it would hold hearings on the bill. Civil rights supporters knew that the committee would not have scheduled the hearings unless it was planning to give the bill a rule and thereby clear the way for floor action.

ANTICLIMAX

Since there was universal recognition that the public proceedings before the Rules Committee would be an empty formality rather than real drama, the star characters did not feel impelled to perform with much verve. Celler contented himself with a warning that the rest of the country could not "supinely and pusillanimously" wait for the southern states to insure Negro voting rights; Colmer of Mississippi reiterated the familiar charge that Celler was abusing the South just to gain favor with Negro voting blocs in the North; and Chairman Smith, using a tested metaphor, asserted that the liberals were "forging manacles" for the South.

Two weeks after the open hearing, the Rules Committee took the action that had been predicted. With the discharge petition lacking only nine of the necessary signatures, Halleck allowed Republicans on the committee to join the four northern Democrats in sending the bill to the floor. In this way, he tried to steal at least some of the thunder from the Democrats and make it possible to argue that it was Republicans who had brought civil rights before the House. Every one of Halleck's followers on the committee came to the aid of his party. The vote to grant a rule to the bill was 7 to 4, with only the Democrats from the South in dissent. The committee also defeated a southern effort to prohibit floor amendments.

Acting for the committee, Colmer reported to the House the ground rules under which H.R. 8601 would be considered. Fifteen hours were to be allotted for general debate. Afterward, members could offer amendments from the floor. The House rule barring those that were not germane to the bill would be in force, but the committee insulated one particular amendment from this type of challenge: the Rogers proposal for referees.

By a vote of 312–93, the House accepted these conditions, and its civil rights debate began. As chairman of the committee that had reported out the civil rights bill, Celler made the formal motion for the House to "resolve itself into the Committee of the Whole House on the State of the Union for the consideration of the bill (H.R. 8601) to enforce constitutional rights, and for other purposes."

IN 1960, THE STRUGGLE to free civil rights legislation from the Rules Committee had not taken place until after the Senate was already immobilized by the southern filibuster. The situation in 1964 was precisely the reverse, and the tussle with the Rules Committee took place at a much earlier stage.

The first round involved an effort to persuade Chairman Smith that he should schedule hearings on sending the bill to the floor. Once again the threat of discharge was used. With Republicans almost as reluctant to sign the petition as they had been in 1960, the pressure was on the Democrats to provide the overwhelming majority of the names that were needed.

From the beginning it was stressed that President Johnson was sympathetic to the discharge attempt. Because of this, the task of rounding up signatures was considerably easier than it had been in 1960. Nor was Johnson's support merely verbal. More than a few of the "holdouts" heard directly from him. Each day, in fact, the President was briefed on who had signed the petition so that he would know which members still needed a personal telephone call. On the first day, 110 Democrats signed, in addition to 20 Republicans. Seventeen more members added their names on the next day, and on the day that followed the signatures mounted steadily toward the magic number that was anathema to Congressman Smith. At the same time, Smith's old friend on the committee, Clarence J. Brown (R., O.), began pressing him to end his obstructionism.

The Virginian saw the handwriting on the wall. To the vast relief of the Administration and its allies, he announced that he had decided to schedule hearings after all. As it turned out, however, the apparent capitulation really represented little more than a shift in tactics. Smith's new plan was to see to it that the hearings dragged on interminably, thus blocking House action just as effectively as if they were not held at all.

For a time the strategy seemed to be succeeding. The chairman and his fellow southerners never ran out of questions for Celler and the other congressmen who came before the committee to ask that the bill be cleared. After eight days of hearings, only eight witnesses had been heard.

There was, however, one way in which Smith might be thwarted. Under the rules, any three members of his committee could threaten him with a procedure that would effectively take control of the committee away from him as far as the civil rights bill was concerned. They could do this by making a formal request that a committee meeting be called to make a decision whether or not the bill should be given a green light. The chairman would have only three days in which to act on the request. If he granted it, the meeting would have to take place within seven days; if he denied it or took no action at all, a majority of the committee members could then call the meeting themselves.

With a bipartisan group on the committee firmly resolved on this admittedly extreme course of action, Smith surrendered and announced to the House leadership that no such extraordinary measures would be required. The committee would go into executive session on January 30th and vote the same day on a rule providing for immediate debate on the House floor and for final action no later than February 11.

Politicians may violate pledges made to their constituents, but they seldom break promises to one another. True to his word, Smith allowed the committee to take a vote on the day he had specified. The result was not even close. By a margin of 11 to 4, the committee agreed to send the civil rights bill to the floor. There, in accordance with normal practice in the House, it would be considered first in the Committee of the Whole.

Committee of the Whole

THE COMMITTEE OF THE WHOLE is a device that the House uses to expedite its business and permit wide participation in debate. It means that the entire membership of the House sits as a committee to consider in detail all aspects of a bill. A casual visitor in the gallery would find it difficult to determine whether he is watching the House or the Committee of the Whole. There are only two visible differences: when the House resolves itself into the Committee of the Whole, the mace is removed from its mounting, and the Speaker is supplanted as presiding officer by a member of his choice.

There was a time when the Committee of the Whole was employed only for strictly financial legislation. Today, however, it is used during approximately 90 per cent of each session. It is difficult to exaggerate its importance. The most detailed consideration of legislation generally takes place during its sessions. It is then that amendments are considered and votes taken on the various sections of a bill. When the House itself reconvenes, it merely decides whether to accept or reject the bill that the committee has produced.

One reason the Committee of the Whole can function more smoothly than the House is its relatively lenient quorum rule. For regular House proceedings, the presence of a majority of the membership is required; by contrast, 100 representatives suffice for the committee to function. Some time is conserved also by the elimination of roll call votes.[47] In addition, only one speaker may be heard on each side of an amendment, and neither of the two may hold the floor for more than five minutes.

But debate as extensive as it is sharp can take place even when the committee is operating under this five-minute rule. For the absence of any ceiling on the number of amendments that may be offered makes it possible for congressman after congressman to employ a simple and amiable subterfuge: the offering of a "*pro forma* amendment." This means that a member wishing to comment on a section of the bill that has already been debated by two speakers may offer an amendment ostensibly designed to "strike out the last word" of the section under consideration. By using this artifice, he wins the right to speak for five minutes on the substantive issue. The *pro forma* amendment he has offered is, of course, not even put to a vote.

Streamlined debate is not the only quality that recommends the Committee of the Whole to many congressmen. The fact that record votes are not permitted may enable a member to delude his constituents as to the role he is playing. Although a bill has strong backing in a congressman's district, he can safely support an amendment that would cripple it, for no official tabulation of that vote will be made. Then, when the Committee of the Whole rises and the House itself takes a roll call vote on the entire bill, he can vote in favor of final passage and thus convince his constituents that he is really their representative.[48]

---

47 When the House, rather than the Committee of the Whole, is meeting, the demand of one-fifth of a quorum is sufficient to order "the yeas and nays." The average roll call vote takes more than thirty minutes, for after the names of the 435 representatives have been called once, the names of members who did not respond are read a second time.

48 Some have attempted to defend such camouflage on grounds supposedly in line with the political philosophy of Edmund Burke. The English conservative did argue that a legislator must not allow his constituents to determine his actions. But that argument does not justify depriving constituents of the opportunity to examine a congressman's voting record for the sake of determining whether to return him to office.

In spite of the differences between the House and the Committee of the Whole, there is one all-important similarity. Both are bound by the rule of germaneness. Unlike the Senate, where riders are somewhat commonplace, the House prohibits amendments not relevant to the purposes of a bill. Power to decide questions of germaneness rests with the presiding officer. Since the strategy of the liberals revolved around the offering of floor amendments to H.R. 8601, it was evident that the congressman whom Speaker Rayburn would select to preside over the Committee of the Whole during the civil rights debate would be in a commanding position.

MR. CHAIRMAN

Rayburn's choice was Francis E. Walter of Pennsylvania. Congressman Walter was best known as the controversial chairman of the House Committee on Un-American Activities. A less publicized fact about him was his close personal friendship with the Speaker. Walter even cherished the hope that someday Rayburn might designate him as his heir. He was, after all, one of the rare northerners with political ideas acceptable to the South. Who could better mediate between the sections of a party divided against itself?

With Walter in the chair, the Committee of the Whole began its general debate on the civil rights bill. In conformity with House practice, the time allotted by the Rules Committee—fifteen hours—was divided equally between supporters and opponents of the measure. Celler, as chairman of the committee that reported the bill, and McCulloch, as ranking minority member, controlled this time. Accordingly, they could select the representatives who would take part in the debate and decide how much time each would have. Custom dictated that Celler and McCulloch, in apportioning the available time, should favor their Judiciary Committee colleagues. Only after all the committee members desiring to participate had been heard would other representatives obtain the floor.

Celler, who was the first to speak, delivered something of an invocation. He began:

Mr. Chairman, I think of the whole world, with little children yet to be born. They will enter into life with sweet and innocent ignorance . . . and early in childhood they will meet with a prickling of the heart and spirit, the ugliness of discrimination.

Does it have to be? No. We can—if only we wish it—erase that ugliness. . . .

As nature provides that flowers be flowers but not all roses or violets or carnations—so we . . . do not demand that [man] change his creed, his religion—his ultimate of impossibilities, his skin. All cannot be alike.

The different instruments in the orchestra can be played to produce diverse tones but which yet can be blended into a beautiful melody. So we ask that human difference be fused into a harmony to make life bearable.

Minority Leader Halleck had soon had his fill of this style of oratory. He began a probing effort to ascertain how seriously Celler would defend his strengthening amendments. Were they really necessary? Would not the committee bill, supplemented by the provision for voting referees, constitute a sufficiently "meaningful and effective advance"? Celler promptly began to back away. "Of course," he said, "if I cannot get the amendments that I have enumerated included in the bill, I will accept the bill as outlined by the distinguished Minority Leader." Halleck tried to nail the point down. He wanted Celler to agree categorically that H.R. 8601 would be "a very definite advance in the direction of the protection of civil rights." Celler proceeded to retreat still further from his original position. Diluting his earlier insistence that the bill's chief value was as a vehicle for amendments, he conceded: "Of course reasonable men may differ as to whether or not [the provisions of H.R. 8601] are helpful enough. I would say they are helpful."

The indications that Celler no longer intended to fight for a strong bill were ignored by southern congressmen, who continued to act as if compulsory miscegenation were just around the corner. Representative Overton Brooks of Louisiana called the committee bill "as vicious an instrument as I have read since I have been in this Congress." Colmer of Mississippi said that "even in the darkest days of the Reconstruction, the Congress never went as far as the proponents of this legislation, in this 1960 election year, propose to go in this nefarious referee, registrar, or overseer bill, whatever you want to call it." And E. L. Forrester of Georgia thought that the bill, at least in part, was the product of a Communist plot. "This civil rights issue has been built up," he said, "by fat and rich malcontents who have received far more from this grovernment than they ever gave in return, and by do-gooders, unscrupulous politicians, and Communists." Forrester buttressed his opinion that the Communists were partly to blame with an obscure allusion to "the Communist Party platform of 1928."

With the end of the general debate, amendments were in order. The time had come to test the theory that H.R. 8601 could be strengthened on the floor.

As chairman of the Judiciary Committee, Celler was entitled to offer the first amendment. He selected the measure that would create a commission to help eliminate discrimination by government contractors. Congressman Smith, the Rules Committee chairman, was on his feet at once to make a point of order. He said that the amendment was not germane, since it introduced "a subject entirely foreign to the bill, as reported by the committee." Nothing in the committee bill related to the subject of work discrimination, he explained. Celler, supported by McCulloch, attacked this line of reasoning. Germaneness could be determined, he said, only by looking to the "fundamental underlying purpose of the bill." That purpose, according to his understanding, was to provide means to enforce constitutional rights. The government-contract amendment would merely add one more link to a civil rights chain.

Congressman Walter, however, found the argument that Smith had made more persuasive. The Celler amendment, he ruled, dealt with an economic question. The main bill, on the other hand, was designed to preserve "certain rights"—apparently voting rights. As a consequence, the amendment was foreign to the purpose of the bill.

Celler proceeded to appeal the chair's decision to the membership. The House, traditionally reluctant to upset a ruling by its presiding officer, was in no mood to violate that custom.

By a "division" (or standing vote), the Committee of the Whole sustained Walter's decision, 157–67.

The next amendment offered by Celler fared no better. This one would have provided federal grants to assist state and local educational agencies in achieving desegregation. The expected point of order on this occasion was made by a member of the Judiciary Committee, Edwin E. Willis of Louisiana. Willis reminded Chairman Walter of his ruling that the bill under consideration dealt with protection of voting rights. The amendment concerned a quite different subject, he said—"federal aid to education"—and, as a consequence, it was not germane.

Celler challenged the premise of Willis' point of order and the Walter ruling on which it was based. He denied that the principal subject of the bill was voting, and he offered as proof the fact that the Rules Committee had waived all points of order on the referee amendment. If the chief purpose of the bill had concerned voting, he argued, this was an unnecessary gesture, for an amendment *on voting* could never have been thought unrelated to a bill *on voting*. The New York congressman reiterated his point of view that H.R. 8601 dealt with a more general subject than voting—the enforcement of constitutional rights. "This amendment," he said, "merely adds another proposition whereby a remedy is provided to enforce a constitutional right, and therefore it is germane." Once again, McCulloch supported him. But the two of them made no headway.

In ruling the second Celler amendment out of order, Walter noted that it concerned education. Had the proposal been introduced as a separate bill, he said, it would have been referred to the Committee on Education and Labor, not the Judiciary Committee. "Therefore," he concluded, "under an abundance of precedent, the chair holds that the amendment offered by the gentleman from New York is not germane because it seeks to introduce a subject matter which would have been referred to a committee other than the one reporting the pending bill."

More than a week later, Celler tried again. This time he introduced a measure to abolish the poll tax. Certainly no one could maintain that *this* proposal had nothing to do with voting. But Walter shifted his ground and sustained another point of order made by Smith. The poll tax could be abolished only through a constitutional amendment, he ruled, not by means of simple legislation; "the proper vehicle" was not being employed to meet the question. There might have been irony in Walter's use of the word "vehicle." To Celler, H.R. 8601 had once been a vehicle into which would be loaded a variety of remedies designed to bring relief to the Negro. As things were turning out, the vehicle was still empty.

Celler's final effort fared no better than its predecessors. Shortly after the poll tax ruling, he introduced the most significant amendment of all—Part III. The inevitable point of order was made by Congressman Willis, and the inevitable ruling followed. Since the amendment "goes away beyond" the right to vote, asserted Walter, it was not germane to the bill.

Neither of the two final rulings was even challenged. The House was clearly not planning to expand the modest dimensions of the administration bill as supplemented by the referee provision. Walter privately expressed the view that all along Celler knew his amendments would be overruled. His action in introducing them was designed merely "to make a record."

A DANGEROUS PRECEDENT

The rulings against Celler's amendments had destroyed all hope of improving the bill. They had even forced the liberals to give up some ground, for from the civil rights standpoint the ruling that only a constitutional amendment could eliminate the poll tax was dangerous. It might be applied to other civil rights proposals, and thus prevent them from becoming law unless they could win acceptance as constitutional amendments.[49]

Earlier in the year there had been at least one indication that Congress inclined toward imposing the complicated amend-

---

49 The Constitution ordains a difficult, two-stage method by which amendments must be approved. First the amendment must be *proposed;* then it must be *ratified.* Although amendments may be proposed by a convention requested by the legislatures of two-thirds of the states, that method has never been used. All

ment procedure. In February, the Senate tabled a proposal by Javits of New York that the poll tax be outlawed by statute, and approved instead a joint resolution submitting to the states a constitutional amendment to eliminate it. The amendment contained two other provisions. One would authorize governors to make temporary appointments to the House of Representatives should a catastrophe decimate its membership, and the other would award the right to vote in presidential elections to residents of the District of Columbia. The House, too, adopted the resolution, but only after its Judiciary Committee had subjected it to a double amputation. The sections dealing with the poll tax and with the emergency appointment of representatives were eliminated. Only the provision modifying the disfranchisement of the National Capital remained.[50] Some liberal members defended the action of the committee. Insistence on the anti-poll tax feature, they said, would have sentenced the entire measure to death, either in the Rules Committee or on the floor.[51] The chairman of the Judiciary Committee pledged to work in the next Congress for a prohibition of the poll tax.[52]

---

24 of the amendments that are now part of the Constitution have instead originated through a two-thirds vote in each house of Congress. Once an amendment has been formally proposed, it is submitted to the states for consideration. Again there are two alternative procedures available. Congress may submit the amendment to conventions in the fifty states, or it may permit the decision to be made by the state legislatures. Except in the case of the Twenty-first Amendment, which repealed Prohibition, the convention method has never been prescribed. Whichever procedure is selected, ratification by three-fourths of the states is necessary for the amendment to be incorporated into the Constitution.

50 In this form, the measure was submitted to the states and was ratified as the Twenty-third Amendment.

51 Actually, only four states—Alabama, Mississippi, Texas, and Virginia—still required the payment of a poll tax. In the Senate it was a southerner—Spessard L. Holland of Florida—who led the effort to outlaw it. On the vote, two of his southern colleagues joined him. Liberals supported the amendment despite their fear, as expressed by Javits, that "we're setting a precedent that all action in this area must be done by constitutional amendment."

52 As it turned out, the next Congress did approve a constitutional amendment to abolish the poll tax in federal elections, and submitted it to the states. The NAACP opposed the amendment, on the theory that it would establish a precedent for handling civil rights through constitutional revision, instead of through simple legislation. The measure was ratified by the states, however, and became the Twenty-fourth Amendment. In 1965, liberals tried to add to the Voting Rights bill a ban on the poll tax in *state* elections, too, but the effort failed.

Decision in the House

THE FATE that had befallen Celler's four amendments almost overtook the administration's referee plan as well. Its nick-of-time rescue contained elements of both melodrama and farce.

Liberal congressmen, never happy about the original Rogers plan, had been greatly disturbed by the alterations it had undergone before assuming legislative form. They viewed one of these changes as particularly damaging: the provision that even after a court had found the existence of a pattern or practice of discrimination, a Negro could not apply to a referee until he had first tried again to register with the appropriate state officials. Defenders of this arrangement said it would give the state a fair opportunity to correct its errors and thus avert further proceedings. Its detractors noted, however, that many southern Negroes, not accustomed to press a white man after he had once refused a request, would resign themselves to disfranchisement rather than risk antagonizing a state official. In addition to this criticism, liberals also deplored the fact that the new draft did not empower the judge to supervise the counting of votes. They feared that, without such supervision, the ballots of qualified Negroes might be disregarded.

Their doubts about the referee plan stronger than ever, some liberal Democrats decided to put forward as an alternative a new version of Senator Hennings' proposal for enrollment officers. This was laid before the House by Congressman Robert W. Kastenmeier of Wisconsin. The plan modified the Hennings formulation, but not significantly. There were only two changes: the federal procedure could be set in motion by the Civil Rights Commission, as well as by the Attorney General; and the President would have more leeway in deciding whether enrollment officers were needed.

STRANGE BEDFELLOWS

Many supporters of a strong bill saw the Kastenmeier amendment as their final opportunity to invigorate the voting-rights provision. But the southerners, too, looked with favor upon its introduction, since it presented a heaven-sent opportunity for attempting to erase *any* voting provision from the civil rights bill. They came within a hair's breadth of succeeding in the attempt.

The principal voting measure before the House was the original referee plan (the only amendment to H.R. 8601 to which the Rules Committee had granted privileged status). It had been introduced by Congressman John V. Lindsay of New York. The *revised* referee draft—the one that would make Negroes try again to register with state officers—had been offered by McCulloch as a substitute for the Lindsay amendment. Technically, therefore, Kastenmeier would have to present his draft as an *amendment* to the McCulloch *substitute* for the original referee *plan*.

Several votes would thus have to be taken. The first question before the House would be whether to abandon referees in favor of enrollment officers. On this question, the southerners decided, they would join the liberal Democrats in support of the stronger Kastenmeier proposal. Their votes, added to those of congressmen genuinely in favor of the stronger plan, would be sufficient to scuttle the referee idea.

But the provision for enrollment officers would still not have been given a final stamp of approval. There would have to be yet another vote (on whether to adopt it as a substitute for the Lindsay amendment). On *this* question, the southerners planned to vote in the negative—and they expected almost all the Republicans to join them. (Since the Kastenmeier-Hennings measure had been stamped as a Democratic bill, Republicans would probably prefer no voting provision at all if the enrollment officers plan was the only one available.) With Republicans and southerners standing together, the plan for enrollment officers would be beaten, and voting would not even be mentioned in the bill.

Proponents of strong legislation were completely in the dark concerning this Machiavellian strategy when the first vote was taken—on whether to supplant referees with enrollment officers. After the liberals had been counted, the southerners, led by Congressman Smith, rose as one man and joined the astonished northerners "in support" of enrollment officers. The result was that the Kastenmeier plan was approved, 152–128. Round 1 had ended as the southerners had hoped.

The second round was no less successful. Since Kastenmeier's plan had replaced the McCulloch substitute, the question before the House was whether to make it a part of the Lindsay amendment. On this vote, with the line-up virtually identical, enrollment officers were again approved, 179–116.

Now the critical vote took place. The choice was between the enrollment officers plan—and nothing. The southerners joined the Republicans in voting for nothing, and the Kastenmeier plan was defeated, 170–143. There was now no voting rights bill before the House.

The southern parliamentary virtuosity, however, merely achieved a momentary triumph. The Republicans, after all, could not risk the accusation that they had helped southerners to sabotage the voting section. Knowing this, McCulloch proceeded to resuscitate the referee plan. Since it had already been voted down, he could not introduce it except in the guise of a new amendment. Accordingly, he deleted the provision authorizing referees to observe the voting on Election Day.[53] A "new" referee amendment was now on the floor.

A veritable comedy of errors ensued. Due to an innocent mistake, McCulloch sent the uncorrected bill to the rostrum. The measure that the Clerk read, therefore, contained the very lines McCulloch had wanted to eliminate. It was, in fact, iden-

---

[53] This provision had been intended to prevent the turning away of Negroes whose registration had been certified by the court.

tical to the referee plan that had just been rejected. As soon as the southerners became aware of the new opportunity that had been handed them, they pounced. Congressman Oren Harris of Arkansas was on his feet at once to make the point of order that "the Clerk did read the language referred to that the gentleman from Ohio just advised the committee was deleted."

There was little doubt that Harris was right. At this point, however, the leaders of both parties wanted to rescue the referee measure, for neither could afford the consequences of any other course. Chairman Walter, the faithful servant of the leadership during the entire debate, saved the day. He permitted Celler to offer the new McCulloch amendment—with the deletion that had been intended—as a substitute for the unabridged plan read by mistake. The House endorsed it with alacrity.

Although it would be a gross exaggeration to say that the liberals had wrested victory from the jaws of defeat, they were at least *almost* back to where they had started.

OTHER AMENDMENTS

In two respects the liberals did succeed in bolstering the referee procedure. The first one affected cases in which state officials might challenge the right to vote of a Negro who was certified by a referee. To reduce the possibility that resultant delays might continue until after Election Day, James G. O'Hara of Michigan proposed a system of provisional voting. His plan would enable a Negro to vote even though his qualifications had been questioned, but the ballot would not be counted until the challenge had been disposed of.[54]

The O'Hara amendment had a second provision. This one constituted an attempt to regain at least part of the ground that had been lost as a result of the debacle over the Kastenmeier amendment. The lines McCulloch had eliminated in

---

[54] The O'Hara amendment made provisional voting available only if the Negro had filed an application with the referee at least twenty days before the election. In the case of others, it would be for the court to determine whether a ballot should be issued.

order to reintroduce his amendment would have permitted the referee to oversee the casting of votes and the counting of ballots. Without specifically mentioning such a power, the O'Hara amendment provided that the court could authorize the referee "to take any . . . action appropriate or necessary" to carry out his decision. The Committee of the Whole accepted the two-pronged amendment, 188–120. It was an unusual victory for a freshman congressman.

Apart from this, the liberals failed in every effort to strengthen the referee procedure. They did, however, ward off all attempts to weaken it still further.

The anti-civil rights amendment that came closest to adoption was offered by Representative Hamer Budge of Idaho, a Republican member of the Rules Committee. Budge wanted to restrict the use of the referee plan to elections in which federal officials were chosen.[55] This meant that it would cover state elections only if they were held at the same time as federal elections.

From the point of view of both the administration and the northern Democrats, however, the Budge maneuver seemed like an abandonment of one of the principal virtues of the referee proposal—its applicability to *all* elections. Attorney General Rogers immediately wrote to McCulloch:

> It would be sheer sanctimony for the United States, on one hand, to continue to guarantee in its Constitution as it has since March 30, 1870 the right of Negroes to vote without discrimination in all elections, both federal and state, and, on the other hand, ninety years later, in March 1960, to enact legislation which, by failing to enforce the right, clearly implies that Negro voting need not be a reality in state elections.

Despite this appeal, about half the Republicans backed the amendment. Budge was aided further by the fact that the vote took place on a Friday. The imminence of the week-end did

[55] Even so, the plan would have gone further than the recommendation of the Civil Rights Commission, which applied only to federal elections. The Budge plan, on the other hand, protected the right to vote in "any election wherein a federal official is being voted upon."

not thin out southern ranks, but those northerners whom cynics on Capitol Hill refer to as members of the Tuesday-Thursday Club were, as usual, in their home districts (attending to private law practices, campaigning out of season, and the like). This factor helped bring the southern bloc within three votes of winning the fight over the Budge amendment.[56]

After defeating an assortment of additional southern amendments, the Committee of the Whole approached the end of its debate. At least one congressman thought that the vote was coming too soon, for he still did not know what the bill was about. It was Representative Clare Hoffman, Republican of Michigan, who felt that he was being rushed. The *Congressional Record* reproduces his contribution:

MR. HOFFMAN of Michigan. . . . There is a great deal of comment on both sides that there are altogether too many lawyers on this committee which reported the bill. Is there some way, Mr. Chairman, that this bill can be given to us complete before we are called upon to vote upon it?

• • • •

MR. MCCORMACK. . . . I could not advise the gentleman. The gentleman would not take my advice anyway.

MR. HOFFMAN of Michigan. Oh well, I might. I do not follow the Ten Commandments all the way down the line as I should, but you can give me some help.

• • • •

MR. CELLER. We can give you the answers but we cannot give you understanding.

MR. HOFFMAN of Michigan. I thank the gentleman for his courtesy. I acknowledge his superior knowledge. If it is not worth any more than some previous suggestions he has made some might still be in doubt. What did you say, anyway? . . . You have frogged around here so that nobody knows where or for what you stand,

---

[56] Three separate votes were taken on the Budge amendment. At first, Chairman Walter put it to a voice vote, and announced that it had been defeated. Budge then obtained a division, or standing vote, which a single member can force. This gave him only 129 votes, as against 148 in opposition. He then moved for a teller vote, and—upon the agreement of more than one-fifth of a quorum—it was ordered. It was on this last and crucial vote that his defeat was most narrow (137 to 134).

as the gentleman from Virginia [Mr. SMITH] so well pointed out yesterday.

If the Republicans were saddled with Clare Hoffman, the Democrats had their E. L. Forrester. The Georgia congressman delivered a speech in which he: (1) charged that the Civil Rights Commission was doing its best "to see that we mongrelize without too much delay"; (2) said (of the civil rights issue), "This thing stinks; it stinks"; and (3) delivered himself of "one more parting shot":

> I am tired of this helpless Negro stuff I hear so much talk about. They got after me one day about the way I pronounced that word. I never had any trouble with a nigger in my life, but oh, my God, that "neegro," I have had plenty with him. I am tired of this helpless sort of stuff. . . .

Having thus heard from all levels of its membership, the Committee of the Whole finally concluded its deliberations with a prolonged standing ovation to Congressman Walter, who then proceeded to report the bill back to the House with the amendments that had been adopted.

ACTION BY THE HOUSE

Speaker Rayburn, once again in the chair, put to a vote the amendments accepted by the Committee of the Whole. All but one of these were endorsed simultaneously, by voice vote. Congressman McCulloch underlined the importance of the referee provision, however, by requesting that it be voted on separately. It was approved on a division, 225–106, and fared even better when Smith of Virginia demanded a roll call.[57] As the *Congressional Record* noted the action: "The yeas and nays were ordered. The question was taken and there were—yeas 295, nays 124. . . ."

When Rayburn called for the final vote "on the engross-

---

[57] One of the few rules of procedure that the Constitution imposes upon Congress concerns the roll call vote. Article I, Section 5, prescribes that one-fifth of the members present may compel the recording of "the Yeas and Nays of the Members. . . ."

ment [58] and third reading [59] of the bill," however, a Mississippi congressman blocked him by demanding that the engrossed copy be read. That forced definitive action to be postponed until the following day, when the final House vote on H.R. 8601 took place. Against the 311 representatives who voted in favor, there were only 109 in opposition.

The bill that the House approved contained the following:

1. Criminal penalties for obstruction of court orders in school desegregation cases.
2. Criminal penalties for flight from one state to another in order to avoid prosecution for destroying any building.
3. A requirement that state officials retain federal election records for two years and make them available to the Attorney General.
4. A provision for federally subsidized education for children of military personnel in areas where local schools had been closed to avoid desegregation.
5. The voting referee plan.

The *Congressional Record* of March 24 reported briefly: "So the bill was passed."

WHEN THE HOUSE DEBATED what was to become the Civil Rights Act of 1964, conditions were markedly different than in 1960. The goal of the civil rights members this time was not to strengthen an anemic bill, but rather to prevent an already strong bill from being crippled. It was now the southerners, not the liberals, who wanted to undo things. In a legislative chamber

[58] An engrossed bill is the certified copy of the legislation as it has finally been approved by one House of Congress.

[59] The term "reading" is something of a misnomer. Nominally, a bill is subjected to three readings. It is, however, considered to have undergone the first when it is introduced and its title is printed in the *Congressional Record*. The requirement for the second is usually met by reading the individual sections of the bill and opening them to amendment. And the third reading (the one that is followed by the final vote) is usually by title only.

where inertia is the rule, that gave a powerful advantage to the Negro and to those who had made his cause their own.

But more than mere inertia was riding with the committee bill. There was also extremely effective organization on the part of its defenders, especially the members of the Democratic Study Group, who functioned with precision and efficiency not at all characteristic of such independent-minded individuals.

For all practical purposes, the Study Group took over the functions of the regular Democratic whip organization. The party leadership looked on approvingly, for the official whip, Hale Boggs, was from Louisiana, and could expect retribution at the polls for any public actions in support of the bill. During the first day of voting on amendments, the Study Group used an intricate system for keeping an eye on congressmen publicly committed to the civil rights cause. The purpose was to bring these members to the floor for votes on critical amendments and, equally important, to make sure that they voted "right." Friendly lobbying organizations provided the manpower for a network of "spotters," each of whom kept tabs on a group of congressmen. If a "spotter" observed that one of his charges was absent when an important vote was impending, he would leave his seat in the visitors' gallery and telephone his information to a central headquarters in the nearby Congressional Hotel. From that headquarters, the information would immediately be relayed to one of the agents manning phones at various strategic locations in the two House Office Buildings. Within seconds, a runner would be on his way to the office of the absentee to request his presence on the House floor.

As the struggle went on, the Study Group members themselves began to corral truants at decisive points in the voting. And there were even some who were assigned to watch the teller lines to minimize the possibility of either absence or chicanery by those supposedly backing the bill.

Participating in this complex operation were the 79 organizations that were now cooperating in the Leadership Conference on Civil Rights. Representatives of organized labor and of the major religious bodies were particularly helpful in providing the necessary personnel for gallery duty and also for buttonholing members. A southern congressman spoke ruefully about the "cardinals, bishops, elders, stated clerks, common preachers, priests, and rabbis [who had] come to Washington to press for passage of the bill." It was indeed an extraordinary display of political ecumenism.

On the anti-civil rights side, lobbyists of any kind were scarce, and men of the cloth were virtually nonexistent. Only a single well-financed organization was in the field: the Coordinating Committee for Fundamental American Freedoms, which was financed in large measure from the treasury of the State of Mississippi.

In the uneven contest that ensued, the bill that had been reported by the Judiciary Committee was never in real trouble. Almost 100 weakening amendments were turned down. And although a few amendments were adopted, there was not a single occasion on which one opposed by the managers of the bill got through. When the final vote on the bill was taken, the margin for passage was more than 2 to 1, with 290 members in favor and only 130 against. For every Democrat who opposed the bill, there were almost two who supported it, and four Republicans cast votes in favor of the legislation for every one on the other side.

Amendments by Senate Judiciary Committee

IN 1960, as in 1964, the House acted before the Senate. Thus, when H.R. 8601 was transmitted to the Senate, it went as more than a mere "bill." Having been passed by one chamber, it now had the official status of an "act." In the Senate, the bipartisan leaders, Senators Johnson and Dirksen, had been awaiting it with open arms, for it seemed an ideal piece of legislation from their point of view. While following its progress in the House, they had become convinced that the Senate would find it more than palatable. True, the southerners could be expected to fulminate against it, but the provisions it contained were weak enough to guarantee that their opposition would be token. As far as the northern Democrats were concerned, they would probably be easy to mollify: the prospect of being able to celebrate enactment of the second civil rights act in three years might be so attractive that they would fix their interest on what the bill contained, not on what it omitted.

The Majority Leader had no intention of permitting Senator Eastland's Judiciary Committee to bury such an excellent measure.[60] As soon as the legislation reached the upper house, he moved to preclude this possibility by tying the hands of the committee. The Senate, he said, should refer the act to the Judiciary Committee, but with binding instructions that the measure was to be reported back within five days. The committee should not be allowed to inter the legislation.

---

60 When the Senate leadership has the will, it can usually find a way to circumvent a committee. In 1957, for example, the civil rights act passed by the House was placed directly on the Senate Calendar, without even going through the Judiciary Committee; that way, a majority could call it up at any time. Similarly, the committee was bypassed in 1959, when the Civil Rights Commission was given a two-year extension through an amendment added to an appropriation bill passed by the House.

Whenever Eastland's committee was accused of a tendency to sidetrack civil rights measures, the senator from Mississippi would assume an air of injured innocence. On one occasion, he had told Senator Carroll of Colorado, a committee colleague who had complained about the treatment of such legislation, that the Judiciary Committee was confronted with "forty different bills and all kinds of amendments, and . . . we are supposed to meet once a week for an hour and a half, under the rules. How then," he demanded, "can the Senator say there have been dilatory tactics employed in the Committee on the Judiciary?" Carroll replied crisply: "I did not say there were dilatory tactics. That means delaying tactics. I said graveyard tactics."

CUT-OFF DATE

Reacting to Johnson's request that a time limit be imposed on the committee, Eastland again insisted that the only reason there had not yet been any action was that the committee was overburdened. The bill and the amendments, he said, "weigh a pound and a half. . . . You cannot count them. You have to weigh them." He appeared cut to the quick by Johnson's implied motion of no confidence. The procedures advocated by the leader amounted in his eyes to a "legislative lynching." His own recommendation, which surprised no one, was that the Senate should refer the House-passed measure to his Judiciary Committee without instructions. This the Senate, by a 72-to-19 vote, refused to do. Instead, it approved the five-day limit, 86–5.[61]

Johnson wanted so badly to obtain speedy action on the bill that even a single day's delay was more than he could endure. Senate rules require that one day intervene between the first reading of a House-passed bill and its second reading. Only then is the legislation eligible for submission to a committee. Yet the Majority Leader managed to send the civil rights act to

61 A considerable number of southerners deserted Eastland on this vote. Only a few of the diehards—Byrd of Virginia, Ellender of Louisiana, Johnston of South Carolina, and Talmadge of Georgia—supported him.

the Judiciary Committee only an hour after the House had passed it.

This was the sequence of events. Upon reaching the Senate, the bill underwent its first reading. Johnson's attempt to gain unanimous consent for an immediate second reading was thwarted by Russell of Georgia, thus making it necessary for the bill to "lie over" for one "legislative day." But, as Joshua had been able to stop the sun in its tracks, so Johnson knew how to speed it up. Taking advantage of the quaint Senate custom under which any adjournment marks the end of a legislative day,[62] he moved successfully to adjourn for three minutes. As dusk, darkness, and daybreak followed each other in sixty-second intervals, one southern senator was heard to grumble: "This is the shortest night I've ever spent!" The Senate "reconvened" when the three minutes had passed, the bill was read for a second time, and Johnson persuaded his colleagues to refer it to the Judiciary Committee with a cut-off date.

HEARINGS AGAIN

The committee conducted two days of hearings. Most of the time was devoted to testimony by Attorney General Rogers. The cabinet member suggested that the committee consider amending the House bill by restoring two administration proposals which had been erased. One of these would help to defray the cost of developing local desegregation programs, and the other would give statutory recognition to the President's Committee on Government Contracts. But Rogers' chief assistant, who also testified, indicated that the Department of Justice was not very insistent on these provisions. He said that "at this point" the administration preferred the House bill to the Dirk-

---

62 Since an adjournment is needed for a page to be torn from the Senate's calendar, there is often no correspondence between the legislative date and the actual date. On March 8, for example, the Senate was still in the legislative day of February 15, because there had been only recesses, instead of adjournments, between the two dates. The Senate had deprived the southerners of the myriad opportunities to waste time that an adjournment would have opened up to them.

sen draft, although only the latter contained the two items in question. When asked why he made that statement, Walsh replied: "Because [H.R. 8601] has already passed the House and is here; it is that much further ahead than Senator Dirksen's bill."

What the administration valued most in the House-passed bill was the referee plan. In an earlier letter to Dirksen, Rogers had dismissed the enrollment officer alternative as "worthless." It would be almost completely ineffective, he said, because it did not provide a method of enforcement. He went so far as to add that it "would make a farce of any bill which included it." If added to the referee section, it "would not only clutter it up with worthless provisions but would seriously weaken it." [63]

Just as Rogers had a low opinion of the enrollment officer plan, the author of that plan found little of value in Rogers' referee idea. Hennings said that the referee procedure, because it presented virtually limitless opportunities for procrastination, would give scant help to the Negro. At the same time, he thought that it would be unfair to southern voting officials. The issuance of court orders against registrars who had discriminated in the past, he explained, would rest on the doubtful inference that they necessarily would continue to impede voting in the future. The senator wanted courts to issue injunctions only if there was "a showing that such protection may be needed." [64]

Southern reservations about referees were aired by Senator Ervin. The North Carolinian concentrated his fire on the fact that state registration officials would not be permitted to appear

---

[63] At the hearings, Senator Hennings displayed resentment at the sharp language Rogers had employed. Another senator who considered the Attorney General's literary style unduly flamboyant was Joseph S. Clark of Pennsylvania. He thought that "the intemperate language and the purple adjectives" would have been "more appropriate to a political speech than to a seriously reasoned legal document intended to call the legal views of the Attorney General of the United States to the attention of the Senate."

[64] One reason Hennings had sought an alternative to the referee plan was that its machinery could not be triggered except through a Justice Department suit under the 1957 act. Up to March 1960, Rogers had filed only four such actions.

before referees because of the provision that "the applicant shall be heard *ex parte*." He called this clearly unconstitutional. If the Supreme Court sustained it, he said, the American people would "no longer have the protection of a written Constitution." [65]

Following the statement by Ervin, Carroll of Colorado criticized the referee plan as being too weak, and then John L. McClellan of Arkansas denounced it as being too strong. If the Administration had deliberately set out to demonstrate that its approach was a middle-of-the-road compromise between two extremes, it could hardly have done better.

EXECUTIVE SESSION

Upon the conclusion of its public hearings, the Judiciary Committee met in executive session to take action on the House bill. In the course of its deliberations, it agreed to recommend ten substantive changes. Not a single section of the measure that had been passed by the House emerged completely unscathed from the barrage of amendments.

The most far-reaching amendment approved by the committee concerned the nature of the hearings to be conducted by a voting referee. The House had decided that the proceedings should be *ex parte,* in order to avoid the kind of hearing that might frighten away a Negro from even *trying* to assert his legal rights. The committee, however, by a 7-to-6 vote, accepted an amendment introduced by Senator Estes Kefauver of Tennessee. It provided that the hearing was to be held in a public place, with two days' notice given to the state or county registrar so that he could attend with counsel.

A second major amendment that the committee adopted was intended to broaden the provision punishing the obstruction of court-ordered school desegregation. The committee decided that the law should cover court orders in any type of case.

Two of the other amendments were designed to avoid placing

---

[65] Rogers shared none of Ervin's apprehensions. He noted that although state officials could not be heard by the referee, they could later testify "before the judge, when the judge makes the decision. . . ."

an unnecessarily heavy financial burden on local communities. For this purpose, the committee thought that states should be required to preserve election records for only 22 months instead of two years. Since elections are held every other year, this would give communities enough time to empty ballot boxes and prepare them for re-use, instead of being compelled to buy new ones. The other amendment that was inspired by considerations of economy would allow Justice Department officials to examine election records only at the place where they were regularly stored; the Attorney General could not ask that the voluminous documents be transported elsewhere for scrutiny.

In addition to these points, the committee eliminated the provision that would make it a federal offense merely to threaten a bombing or initiate a false bomb scare. The Justice Department favored this deletion, since it did not want to deprive state police of jurisdiction over what it considered to be essentially local crimes.

The committee rejected several of the amendments that were offered. One was a proposal by Senator Keating of New York that Congress express its agreement with the Supreme Court's condemnation of public school segregation. This was defeated, 10–3. Another suggestion by Keating, to authorize federal aid for communities desegregating their schools, failed by one vote. Hennings' effort to combine his enrollment officers procedure with the referee plan was dismissed, 8–6. Finally, the committee refused to modify the bill's requirement that a Negro seeking the protection of a federal referee would first have to prove he had been turned away by a state registration official.

Assessing the net effect of the amendments, the liberal *Washington Post* was pleasantly surprised that the committee had been so "restrained in its undercutting of the . . . bill." But three senators, including Hennings, were sufficiently disappointed to file a detailed minority report when the committee sent the revised bill to the floor.

In their dissenting opinion, the senators urged acceptance of the plan for enrollment officers as a complement to the referee method. They wanted to leave to the President and Attorney

1 ~~and copying at the principal office of the person upon whom~~
2 ~~such demand is made or at an office of the United States~~
3 ~~attorney in the district in which such records or papers are~~
4 ~~located.~~
5 SEC. ~~305~~ *304.* Unless otherwise ordered by a court of the
6 United States, neither the Attorney General nor any em-
7 ployee of the Department of Justice, nor any other repre-
8 sentative of the Attorney General, shall disclose any record
9 or paper produced pursuant to this title, or any reproduction
10 or copy, except to Congress and any committee thereof,
11 governmental agencies, and in the presentation of any case
12 or proceeding before any court or grand jury.
13 SEC. ~~306~~ *305.* The United States district court for the
14 district in which a demand is made pursuant to section 303,
15 or in which a record or paper so demanded is located, shall
16 have jurisdiction by appropriate process to compel the pro-
17 duction of such record or paper.
18 SEC. ~~307~~ *306.* As used in this title, the term "officer of
19 election" means any person who, under color of any Federal,
20 State, Commonwealth, or local law, statute, ordinance, regu-
21 lation, authority, custom, or usage, performs or is authorized
22 to perform any function, duty, or task in connection with
23 any application, registration, payment of poll tax, or other
24 act requisite to voting in any general, special, or primary
25 election at which votes are cast for candidates for the office

Page of 1960 House-passed bill, amended by Senate Judiciary Committee. Line running through word indicates committee dropped it. New material appears in italics.

General the choice of the more appropriate method in each case that would arise. It was evident, however, that the authors of the minority views hoped that the referee alternative would be used infrequently, if at all. Its legalistic approach, they said, would entail "endless pitfalls and shortcomings," and would place in the courts the responsibility for registration and election, although that was not properly a judicial function.

Decision in the Senate

THE MINORITY REPORT filed by the liberals apparently influenced few votes. When Hennings offered his plan for enrollment officers to the Senate as a whole, it was tabled, 58–26.

On the very first day of the floor debate, however, virtually all the Judiciary Committee's amendments were adopted. The only stumbling block was Kefauver's successful attempt in committee to modify the *ex parte* character of the referee proceedings. His amendment, as approved by the committee, read as follows:

> The hearing shall be held in a public office. The referee shall give the county or state registrar two days' written notice of the time and place of the hearing and such state or county registrar, or his counsel, shall have the right to appear and make a transcript of the proceedings.

Floor debate indicated that there was considerable doubt as to the meaning of the word "appear." Would it not give the registrar the right to cross-examine the Negro and thus, conceivably, intimidate him? Senator Carroll, who had cast the deciding vote for the amendment in committee, revealed that he for one had intended no such result. His only desire had been to dispel any implication that the hearing was to be clandestine. To eliminate the ambiguity that had arisen, he took the floor to recommend a rewording. The amendment he now favored would provide that the Negro was to be heard *ex parte*, but in proceedings that would be open to the public. The Senate ratified the change, 69–22.

Only one other alteration was made in the bill reported by the Judiciary Committee. By a vote of 79 to 12, the Senate accepted an amendment offered by Dirksen. It would allow provisional voting only in situations where the court found that a Negro met the state's electoral qualifications.

Although the Senate accepted only the Carroll and Dirksen amendments to the bill reported out by the committee, it considered a wide variety of others. There was little support for those that were put forward by southerners to weaken the bill. For example, an attempt by Ervin to restrict referees to congressional elections received only sixteen votes, and no more than eighteen senators backed an amendment by Allen J. Ellender of Louisiana to tear up the entire referee plan. The showing of the liberals was slightly more impressive: Part III attracted 34 votes, and an amendment offered by Senator Javits to establish a permanent Commission on Equal Job Opportunity received 38 of the 86 votes cast.

FOLLOW THE LEADER

The Javits amendment was rushed to a vote by Johnson over its sponsor's protest that he was not yet prepared to call it up. When Javits asked for more time, Johnson exploded, as he had never done at the southerners:

> Mr. President, I do not want to yield my majority leader duties to the Senator from New York—yet . . . [We] . . . sit and sit and sit, and wait and wait and wait, and listen and listen and listen; and if the Senator from New York is not prepared on his contract provision now, I do not know when he will be prepared. . . . The last place in the world I expected to get the "dagger" from was the Senator from New York. . . .

Javits was enraged at the baiting. Told that he had agreed to be ready for a vote after thirty minutes, he categorically denied having made such a promise. His version of what had supposedly taken place was so bitter that it never appeared in the *Congressional Record*. This is a close paraphrase of what he said: [66]

---

[66] The author was a witness to the exchange.

The Majority Leader has a very interesting habit. He will approach a senator and tell him what he thinks should be done about a particular issue. And if the senator doesn't jump up and down, wave his hands, and shout, "No! No!" the Majority Leader will later assert, with complete conviction, that the senator was enthusiastically in agreement with his point of view.

On the same day—one senator noted pointedly for the record that it was April Fool's Day—Johnson's Republican counterpart launched an attack on another liberal, Joseph S. Clark of Pennsylvania. The incident began with a complaint by Clark that the time at his disposal had been severely restricted by a unanimous consent agreement made while he was absent from the chamber. When Dirksen challenged the insinuation that this had been deliberately done, Clark replied: "The senator from Illinois is completely incorrect. While he was out of the room, the junior senator from New York . . ." Dirksen would not let him finish. "I make a point of order," he shouted, "I ask that the senator from Pennsylvania take his seat, under the rule." [67] Even when the presiding officer forced Clark to surrender the floor temporarily, Dirksen was not satisfied. "I will not have the senator from Pennsylvania impugn my motives or my conduct on the Senate floor," he thundered. "Otherwise, I will have to assert my privilege right now and shut him off."

After tempers had cooled, Clark said he had been asked whether he still loved the senator from Illinois. "Yes, I still love him," he assured his colleagues.

There was, of course, something other than personal animosity involved in the dispute. Clark was seething because he thought that the leadership was less patient with the amendments of northerners than with those of southerners. He was tired of being told that strengthening the bill might provoke the House Rules Committee to revert to obstructionism. "It would not affect one iota whether the . . . bill . . . would be pickled in conference by the Rules Committee," he said.

---

67 The rule Dirksen was invoking provides: "No Senator in debate shall, directly or indirectly, by any form of words impute to another Senator or to other Senators any conduct or motive unworthy or unbecoming a Senator." A member who is called to order for violating the rule must be seated until the Senate allows him to proceed.

APPOMATTOX IN REVERSE

As the battle approached its conclusion, Senator Harry F. Byrd of Virginia was ready to announce who had won. "In the main," he told the Senate, "the result has been a victory for the South. . . . To paraphrase Sir Winston Churchill, so few at such great odds have done so much for so many." He explained that the most objectionable features of the administration's bill had been eliminated, and that some of the remaining provisions had been modified "in measurable degree." Senator Clark, acknowledging the southern triumph, declared:

> Surely in this battle on the Senate floor the roles of Grant and Lee at Appomattox have been reversed. The eighteen implacable defenders of the way of life of the Old South are entitled to congratulations from those of us they have so disastrously defeated. To be sure, at critical moments, they had the assistance of the President of the United States, the Attorney General, the Minority Leader, and the Majority Leader.

The two leaders, however, were busy congratulating each other. "I salute the Majority Leader of the U.S. Senate," declaimed Dirksen. "I am particularly grateful to the distinguished Minority Leader . . . for his complete cooperation at all times," reciprocated Johnson.

Clark called the legislation that had been developed "a weak Republican bill, watered down by southern and southwestern Democratic votes." It had been weakened to such an extent, he warned, that he was not entirely certain he could support it on final passage. His words were strong:

> There is a real question in my mind whether the bill as it stands today in the Senate is anything more than a sham which will fool some people into believing that we have done something for the disfranchised citizens who have been discriminated against for years, but which in fact is not going to do them any good at all.

The last southern attempt to win a total victory and bury the entire bill was a motion by Eastland for recommittal to his Judiciary Committee. Dirksen's request that this be tabled was approved, 70–19, with only Dennis Chavez of New Mexico joining the southern bloc.

On April 8, with all the preliminaries out of the way, the Senate was ready to take a final vote on the bill as a whole. The southerners made no effort to prevent action by means of a filibuster. They were content simply to register their opposition when the roll was called. The vote in favor of passing the bill was 71 to 18.

IN 1964, THE EXUBERANCE of the liberals was unrestrained as the Senate prepared to vote on final passage of the civil rights bill. Four years earlier, the mountain had labored mightily but had been able to bring forth only a mouse. Now, by contrast, there was a product that no one had to apologize for.

The final vote in the Senate showed that a remarkable consensus had built up in favor of the legislation. With all 100 senators voting, a full 73 of them registered approval of the bill. The only Democrats among the remaining 27 were the unreconstructed southerners and 3 senators from border states. The rest of the negative votes were cast by Senator Goldwater and five of his Republican colleagues who were supporting his campaign for the presidential nomination. One year to the day after the late President Kennedy had submitted his civil rights bill to Congress, decisive Senate action had finally come.

A Bill Becomes a Law

BECAUSE THE SENATE had made changes in 1960 in the bill passed by the House, the legislation had to be returned to that chamber for further action. In such cases, the two Houses often appoint "managers" to a conference committee, which then tries to hammer out a compromise acceptable to both chambers.[68] In the present instance, however, there was no disposition in the House to resist the Senate's amendments. If only the Rules Committee would cooperate, it would be a simple matter to endorse the changes made by the Senate and forward the bill to the President. Although Chairman Smith took his time about calling the Rules Committee together, he knew that there was no hope of blocking the measure. The southerners were sure to be outvoted by a combination of northern Democrats and those Republicans willing to accept the modest bill that had been produced.

At a public hearing of the Rules Committee, Smith seemed anything but upset at the prospect of his "defeat." Holding court in a crowded little committee room, he posed for photographers, commented sarcastically on Congressman Celler's absence, and indulged in homespun badinage with any reporter who would encourage him. When it became evident that no witness would appear, he ordered the room cleared, and the committee went into executive session. A few minues later, the doors were opened and the members announced the news. Seven of them had voted for the resolution to concur in the amendments that the Senate had added. The only opposition had come from Representative Budge of Idaho and the three southern Democrats who were present.

Congressman Richard Bolling of Missouri, a Democratic member of the Rules Committee, rose in the House on April 21 to call up House Resolution 503 and ask for its immediate consideration. The clerk read its text:

> *Resolved,* That immediately upon the adoption of this resolution, the bill H.R. 8601, with the Senate amendments thereto, be, and the same is, taken from the Speaker's table, to the end that the Senate amendments be, and the same are, hereby agreed to.

At once Congressman Celler took the floor and claimed paternity of the new-born law—"the Celler-McCulloch bill," as

[68] Typically, the managers are the senior members of the House and Senate committees that handled the bill originally. The conference method thus augments significantly the power of the chairman and senior members of each standing committee.

he called it. He consoled the Negro with the thought that "a small key can sometimes open a big door." Access to the ballot, he said, would give the Negro "a shield to forfend wicked officials, and a sword to fight for his unalienable rights—life, liberty, and the pursuit of happiness." McCulloch of Ohio agreed that the bill was "the golden mean." The House, he said, was enjoying one of its "finest hours." To Colmer of Mississippi, the bill was something different—"a bid for the minority bloc vote," "a vicious attack . . . upon the fundamental structure of our country," and discrimination "against white people in favor of Negroes."

It was, however, too late for speeches to have any effect. When "the previous question on the resolution" was moved by Congressman Bolling and the Speaker ordered a roll call vote, the House overwhelmingly accepted the Senate's amendments, 288–95.[69]

With both Houses of Congress having approved H.R. 8601, the measure was printed on parchment and signed by Speaker Rayburn and Vice President Nixon (in his capacity as President of the Senate). It was now an "enrolled bill." In this form, it was sent to the White House, where President Eisenhower signed it into law on May 6. The Civil Rights Act of 1960 had become Public Law 86-449.

THE LAST ACT in the 1964 drama followed a somewhat similar script. Once again the only serious problem related to the Rules Committee. Unless that committee acquiesced, the House would have no chance to accept the Mansfield-Dirksen substitute as the Senate had done.

69 Through a device known as "pairs," 22 other congressmen recorded their position. The pairing procedure allows a member who must be absent to record the vote he would otherwise cast. To do so, he enters into an advance agreement with a colleague who favors the opposing viewpoint. Both members agree to refrain from voting even if the anticipated absence does not materialize. Such "live pairs" differ from three other types of agreements that do not reveal how the parties to them would have voted. The "general," "further notice," and "session" pairs do little more than announce the presumably unavoidable absences of those who have entered into them.

Chairman Smith did not exactly say no; he merely made no move to call a meeting of the committee.

To prod Smith into action, three of his colleagues decided to use the same device that they had threatened him with at an earlier stage. They filed a formal request for the committee to be called together, thus confronting Smith with the choice of scheduling the meeting himself or having it done for him by his determined colleagues. The chairman chose the lesser evil and called the meeting. That way, he at least avoided a formal rebuff. But an even greater rebuff was in prospect for him, and he could do nothing to avoid that one.

The bitter medicine was administered to Smith in two almost equally obnoxious doses. First, the committee acted to prevent him from filibustering to delay a vote on actually clearing the bill. Shortly after the session began, a member who favored the bill moved that a final vote be taken by 5 o'clock of the same day on reporting the necessary resolution to the House floor. When Smith ruled the motion out of order on the ground that it could be offered only during an executive session, the committee promptly voted to go into executive session, and soon afterward the motion to impose the deadline was carried easily. Then the resolution itself was approved.

But the unkindest cut of all was still to come. Although Smith had been resigned to the decision sending the bill to the floor, he had expected to be in charge of presenting the necessary resolution to the House. That would enable him to delay for a full ten days: he would have three days to present the resolution to the Speaker and then a full week more before he would be compelled to call it up for action. The delay would mean that the critical vote might be put off until just before the Republican National Convention, when members of the House would be chafing to get away. The chairman was foiled again, however, when the committee voted not to

Eighty-sixth Congress of the United States of America

AT THE SECOND SESSION

Begun and held at the City of Washington on Wednesday, the sixth day of January, one thousand nine hundred and sixty

An Act

To enforce constitutional rights, and for other purposes.

Be it enacted by the Senate and House of Representatives of the United States of America in Congress assembled, That this Act may be cited as the "Civil Rights Act of 1960".

TITLE I

OBSTRUCTION OF COURT ORDERS

SEC. 101. Chapter 73 of title 18, United States Code, is amended by adding at the end thereof a new section as follows:

"§ 1509. Obstruction of court orders

"Whoever, by threats or force, willfully prevents, obstructs, impedes, or interferes with, or willfully attempts to prevent, obstruct, impede, or interfere with, the due exercise of rights or the performance of duties under any order, judgment, or decree of a court of the United States, shall be fined not more than $1,000 or imprisoned not more than one year, or both.

"No injunctive or other civil relief against the conduct made criminal by this section shall be denied on the ground that such conduct is a crime."

SEC. 102. The analysis of chapter 73 of such title is amended by adding at the end thereof the following:

"1509. Obstruction of court orders."

TITLE II

FLIGHT TO AVOID PROSECUTION FOR DAMAGING OR DESTROYING ANY BUILDING OR OTHER REAL OR PERSONAL PROPERTY; AND, ILLEGAL TRANSPORTATION, USE OR POSSESSION OF EXPLOSIVES; AND, THREATS OR FALSE INFORMATION CONCERNING ATTEMPTS TO DAMAGE OR DESTROY REAL OR PERSONAL PROPERTY BY FIRE OR EXPLOSIVES

SEC. 201. Chapter 49 of title 18, United States Code, is amended by adding at the end thereof a new section as follows:

"§ 1074. Flight to avoid prosecution for damaging or destroying any building or other real or personal property

"(a) Whoever moves or travels in interstate or foreign commerce with intent either (1) to avoid prosecution, or custody, or confinement after conviction, under the laws of the place from which he flees, for willfully attempting to or damaging or destroying by fire or explosive any building, structure, facility, vehicle, dwelling house, synagogue, church, religious center or educational institution, public or private, or (2) to avoid giving testimony in any criminal proceeding relating to any such offense shall be fined not more than $5,000 or imprisoned not more than five years, or both.

"(b) Violations of this section may be prosecuted in the Federal judicial district in which the original crime was alleged to have been committed or in which the person was held in custody or confinement: *Provided, however*, That this section shall not be construed as indicating an intent on the part of Congress to prevent any State, Territory, Commonwealth, or possession of the United States of any jurisdiction over any offense over which they would have jurisdiction in the absence of such section."

A portion of the "enrolled" copy of Civil Rights Act of 1960

H. R. 8601—7

any extent administered by a person found in the proceeding to have violated subsection (a); and the words 'qualified under State law' shall mean qualified according to the laws, customs, or usages of the State, and shall not, in any event, imply qualifications more stringent than those used by the persons found in the proceeding to have violated subsection (a) in qualifying persons other than those of the race or color against which the pattern or practice of discrimination was found to exist."

(b) Add the following sentence at the end of subsection (c):

"Whenever, in a proceeding instituted under this subsection any official of a State or subdivision thereof is alleged to have committed any act or practice constituting a deprivation of any right or privilege secured by subsection (a), the act or practice shall also be deemed that of the State and the State may be joined as a party defendant and, if, prior to the institution of such proceeding, such official has resigned or has been relieved of his office and no successor has assumed such office, the proceeding may be instituted against the State."

TITLE VII

SEPARABILITY

Sec. 701. If any provision of this Act is held invalid, the remainder of this Act shall not be affected thereby.

Sam Rayburn

Speaker of the House of Representatives.

Richard Nixon

Vice President of the United States and President of the Senate.

Approved—
Dwight D Eisenhower
6 May 1960

with signatures of President and presiding officers of both Houses.

Eighty-eighth Congress of the United States of America

AT THE SECOND SESSION

Begun and held at the City of Washington on Tuesday, the seventh day of January, one thousand nine hundred and sixty-four

An Act

To enforce the constitutional right to vote, to confer jurisdiction upon the district courts of the United States to provide injunctive relief against discrimination in public accommodations, to authorize the Attorney General to institute suits to protect constitutional rights in public facilities and public education, to extend the Commission on Civil Rights, to prevent discrimination in federally assisted programs, to establish a Commission on Equal Employment Opportunity, and for other purposes.

Be it enacted by the Senate and House of Representatives of the United States of America in Congress assembled, That this Act may be cited as the "Civil Rights Act of 1964".

TITLE I—VOTING RIGHTS

SEC. 101. Section 2004 of the Revised Statutes (42 U.S.C. 1971), as amended by section 131 of the Civil Rights Act of 1957 (71 Stat. 637), and as further amended by section 601 of the Civil Rights Act of 1960 (74 Stat. 90), is further amended as follows:

(a) Insert "1" after "(a)" in subsection (a) and add at the end of subsection (a) the following new paragraphs:

"(2) No person acting under color of law shall—

"(A) in determining whether any individual is qualified under State law or laws to vote in any Federal election, apply any standard, practice, or procedure different from the standards, practices, or procedures applied under such law or laws to other individuals within the same county, parish, or similar political subdivision who have been found by State officials to be qualified to vote;

"(B) deny the right of any individual to vote in any Federal election because of an error or omission on any record or paper relating to any application, registration, or other act requisite to voting, if such error or omission is not material in determining whether such individual is qualified under State law to vote in such election; or

"(C) employ any literacy test as a qualification for voting in any Federal election unless (i) such test is administered to each individual and is conducted wholly in writing, and (ii) a certified copy of the test and of the answers given by the individual is furnished to him within twenty-five days of the submission of his request made within the period of time during which records and papers are required to be retained and preserved pursuant to title III of the Civil Rights Act of 1960 (42 U.S.C. 1974–74e; 74 Stat. 88): *Provided, however*, That the Attorney General may enter into agreements with appropriate State or local authorities that preparation, conduct, and maintenance of such tests in accordance with the provisions of applicable State or local law, including such special provisions as are necessary in the preparation, conduct, and maintenance of such tests for persons who are blind or otherwise physically handicapped, meet the purposes of this subparagraph and constitute compliance therewith.

"(3) For purposes of this subsection—

"(A) the term 'vote' shall have the same meaning as in subsection (e) of this section;

"(B) the phrase 'literacy test' includes any test of the ability to read, write, understand, or interpret any matter."

(b) Insert immediately following the period at the end of the first sentence of subsection (c) the following new sentence: "If in any such proceeding literacy is a relevant fact there shall be a rebuttable

The first and last pages of the Civil Rights Act of 1964

H. R. 7152—28

TITLE XI—MISCELLANEOUS

SEC. 1101. In any proceeding for criminal contempt arising under title II, III, IV, V, VI, or VII of this Act, the accused, upon demand therefor, shall be entitled to a trial by jury, which shall conform as near as may be to the practice in criminal cases. Upon conviction, the accused shall not be fined more than $1,000 or imprisoned for more than six months.

This section shall not apply to contempts committed in the presence of the court, or so near thereto as to obstruct the administration of justice, nor to the misbehavior, misconduct, or disobedience of any officer of the court in respect to writs, orders, or process of the court. No person shall be convicted of criminal contempt hereunder unless the act or omission constituting such contempt shall have been intentional, as required in other cases of criminal contempt.

Nor shall anything herein be construed to deprive courts of their power, by civil contempt proceedings, without a jury, to secure compliance with or to prevent obstruction of, as distinguished from punishment for violations of, any lawful writ, process, order, rule, decree, or command of the court in accordance with the prevailing usages of law and equity, including the power of detention.

SEC. 1102. No person should be put twice in jeopardy under the laws of the United States for the same act or omission. For this reason, an acquittal or conviction in a prosecution for a specific crime under the laws of the United States shall bar a proceeding for criminal contempt, which is based upon the same act or omission and which arises under the provisions of this Act; and an acquittal or conviction in a proceeding for criminal contempt, which arises under the provisions of this Act, shall bar a prosecution for a specific crime under the laws of the United States based upon the same act or omission.

SEC. 1103. Nothing in this Act shall be construed to deny, impair, or otherwise affect any right or authority of the Attorney General or of the United States or any agency or officer thereof under existing law to institute or intervene in any action or proceeding.

SEC. 1104. Nothing contained in any title of this Act shall be construed as indicating an intent on the part of Congress to occupy the field in which any such title operates to the exclusion of State laws on the same subject matter, nor shall any provision of this Act be construed as invalidating any provision of State law unless such provision is inconsistent with any of the purposes of this Act, or any provision thereof.

SEC. 1105. There are hereby authorized to be appropriated such sums as are necessary to carry out the provisions of this Act.

SEC. 1106. If any provision of this Act or the application thereof to any person or circumstances is held invalid, the remainder of the Act and the application of the provision to other persons not similarly situated or to other circumstances shall not be affected thereby.

John W. McCormack

Speaker of the House of Representatives.

Carl Hayden

President pro tempore of the Senate.

Lyndon B. Johnson
approved July 2, 1964
Washington, D.C.

as signed into law by President Johnson.

entrust the resolution to him but rather to another member of the committee, Congressman Ray J. Madden (D., Ind.). Smith may have been hurt by the insult, but no remedy was available to him.

Only two days after the Rules Committee had met and voted, the resolution to concur in the Senate substitute came to the floor of the House. The margin by which it was adopted was even wider than the one that had existed when the House had agreed to the bill reported by its own Judiciary Committee. In favor of the resolution were 289 members, even including one from Georgia (Charles L. Weltner, who represented Atlanta). Only 126 votes were cast in opposition.

With this resounding vote of confidence, the bill went to the White House. In a matter of hours, President Johnson had affixed his signature, and the strongest civil rights bill since the Reconstruction was the law of the land.

CONCLUSION

"THE CIVIL RIGHTS ACT OF 1960 isn't worth the paper it's written on." This bitter comment was made, shortly after enactment of the law, by Thurgood Marshall, who argued the School Segregation Cases in the Supreme Court and is now Solicitor General of the United States. Subsequent events did not indicate that Marshall had been guilty of exaggeration. In the 1960 election, no use was made of the referee plan, though it had been heralded as the most important part of the bill. Southern judges were also reluctant to apply the law in 1962. On the few occasions when they did act, Negroes were deterred from using the procedure by the requirement that they would first have to approach local election officials and try to register with them. Considering the amount of time and energy that went into the making of the law and the pressing need that existed for legislative protection of the Negro, the revelation of how weak a statute Congress produced in 1960 was sharply disillusioning.

On the subject of voting, there was also disillusionment after the passage of the Civil Rights Act of 1964. Within months, the failure of the new law to deal effectively with racial disfranchisement had become so glaringly obvious that Congress was once again compelled to grapple with the problem and pass the Voting Rights Act of 1965.

But unlike the 1960 law, the statute passed in 1964 had important provisions on subjects other than voting. There were also sections on discrimination in public accommodations, schools, employment, and programs assisted by the federal government. On these subjects, at least some concrete results could be observed immediately. With respect to public accommodations, for example, there was swift compliance in a large number of southern cities, and at least a dim awareness in the rural areas that defiance could do no more than postpone the inevitable. Of the 1964 law, then, it cannot be said that it "isn't worth the paper it's written on."

What accounted for the palpable difference between 1960 and 1964? What factors operated in 1960 to frustrate the proponents of civil rights at every turn? And why was the importance of these factors diminished in 1964?

There is little doubt that President Eisenhower must shoulder some responsibility for the fact that the Civil Rights Act of 1960 was so weak. Only with the firm support of a President, particularly in his role as party leader, can there ever be a favorable prognosis for liberal legislation in Congress. Mr. Eisenhower, however, chose equivocation and inaction rather than resolute leadership on civil rights. Yet the President's attitude by no means provides the entire explanation for what happened. Even if Mr. Eisenhower had thrown himself wholeheartedly into the struggle, the final outcome might have been much the same, for a powerful conservative coalition was in firm control of Congress.

That coalition had been functioning for more than two decades. Because of its effectiveness, almost any session of Congress furnished examples of legislative measures whose final versions were far different from the bold and original bills they had once been. Moreover, the strength of the coalition was affected only slightly by popular elections, although most Americans believe that these elections determine the political complexion of Congress. For regardless of which party would achieve a formal majority, the reality of power—something very different from the appearance of power—remained in the same hands. Both groups comprising the coalition—the southern Democrats and the right-wing Republicans—generally sought identical goals: an end to positive federal legislation on social and economic issues. The southerners, who desired to defeat or dilute civil rights legislation, and the Republicans, whose principal desire was the scrapping of social welfare proposals, cooperated closely to assure the death of both types of measures.

If it were not for the strangely ambivalent character of the Democratic party, such a peculiar situation could not exist. As Peter Finley Dunne once heard Mr. Dooley say, "Th' dimmy-cratic party ain't on speakin' terms with itsilf." It would be hard to imagine, for instance, two individuals separated more widely by philosophical differences than Paul Douglas and James Eastland. Yet the liberal and the segregationist belong to the same party, and each benefits from the election of the other since both share in the rewards that Democratic control of the Senate brings.

The nature of the Democratic party as an uneasy collaboration of polar opposites has generally led it to exclude from positions of national leadership those individuals with reputations as extremists. Southern segregationists are not nominated for the presidency, yet neither are those men with uncompromisingly liberal records; a racist will never become the Democratic leader in the Senate, but neither will a Wayne Morse. The Democrat who is the ideal leader is one who has learned to subordinate all other values to party unity. On Lyndon Johnson, the mantle of leadership rested comfortably during the fight over civil rights in 1959 and 1960.

Johnson's position as an honest broker did not mean that he could always adopt positions precisely midway between the extremes, or that he could side with the liberals just as frequently as with the conservatives. There is no task more difficult than to convince conservatives that they ought to support positive actions offensive to them; it is far easier to make liberals believe that progress against entrenched social and economic evils must of necessity be slow. Not surprisingly, therefore, Johnson's conception of the middle of the road was considerably to the right of dead center. During the debate in 1960, for example, he concentrated far more on trimming the demands of the liberals than on prodding the southerners. As on many occasions in the past, he worked more closely with Everett Dirksen, the Republican leader in the Senate, than with the civil rights Democrats.

If conservatives benefited from the alliance between Johnson and Dirksen, they were aided even more by another phenomenon: the conservative nature of several important congressional procedures.

Perhaps the most conspicuous example of the conservative bias in Congress was the Rules Committee of the House. When the Republicans held a majority, the conservative domination of this committee was assured, and liberal measures on both economic issues and civil rights scarcely had a chance. The result was not very different, however, when a resurgence of liberalism in the country gave a majority in the House to the Democrats. In the Eighty-sixth Congress, for example, the four conservative Republicans on the committee found to their delight that they had precisely the number of southern Democratic allies they needed to bottle up liberal legislation.

The filibuster was another congressional procedure that was anything but neutral in its political effects. Like the Rules Committee in the House, it had become primarily an instrument of conservative power. It had, in fact, seldom been used successfully for anything except to force the abandonment or emasculation of civil rights proposals.

Although the power of the Rules Committee and the threat of the filibuster were the best known elements of the conservative bias in Congress, they were by no means the only ones. The disproportionate number of southerners at the head of standing committees—almost entirely a product of the seniority system—was at least as important. And even the bare fact that the rules were so cumbersome was significant. The procedures that follow the introduction of a bill and its reference to committee are so formidable that they might well have been devised by men who hated the thought that legislation would ever be enacted. In an age when liberals are insisting that the federal government take positive steps to fashion a more equitable and democratic society, a barrier to all congressional action hurts their cause directly. Conservatives, who demand far less of government, lose little.

The newspaper columnist, Joseph Alsop, has argued that something else was to blame for the civil rights debacle in 1960. The liberals, he says, were both stubborn and inept, and thus did grave damage to their cause. They were "less interested in the dusty legislative process than in striking noble, popular postures." Undoubtedly the liberals did not understand parliamentary procedure as well as the southern conservatives (partly because not too many of them had been in Congress as long). Certainly they had no leaders whose generalship could equal that of Lyndon Johnson, Sam Rayburn, Richard Russell, or Howard Smith. Yet these factors had only slight bearing on the defeat they suffered. Even if they had been past masters of legislative procedure and experts in the art of compromise, they would still have had no chance at all to overcome the awesome power marshalled against them by the conservative coalition.

Although the coalition was far from defunct in 1964, a new condition had arisen that reduced it to impotence. That condition was the increased militance of the Negro protest movement and the threat of ruinous violence created in parts of the Deep South by the intransigence and brutality with which the protest was met. First President Kennedy and then President Johnson, as well as the bipartisan leadership in Congress, came to the conclusion that only a strong civil rights bill could possibly prevent widespread racial bloodshed and utter catastrophe for the nation. Given such bipartisan determination, which was particularly pronounced after the events in Birmingham in the spring of 1963, obstacles in Congress tended to melt away.

It is a sad commentary on the American system of government that the Negro had to go into the streets before anything even approximating serious attention was paid to his legitimate grievances. Those who glorify the system in terms of its responsiveness to the long-range public interest will not find it easy to explain why it required street demonstrations and the imminence of chaos to awaken presidents and congressmen to their responsibilities.

Tragically, the awakening may have come too late. The civil rights movement had built up so much momentum by 1964 that even the new law was seen as not going far enough. The demand, unanswerable in its own terms, was for "freedom now!" Particularly among northern Negroes—for whom the 1964 law did relatively little—pent-up frustrations had combined with rising expectations to create a highly inflammable situation. Understandably, the Negro community in both the North and South was not ready to concede the good faith of the white political elite merely on the basis of a law whose enactment had been compelled by marching feet. Only the most militant tactics had finally persuaded Congress to act. These tactics, it was certain, would be used again and again.

Things might have been very different had Congress moved a little earlier. Even 1960 might not have been too late. The Legislative Branch, however, was immobilized by a combination of factors: a President who was the epitome of complacency; a Senate Majority Leader who sensed no insistent national demand for a strong bill; and congressional procedures, such as the filibuster, that made it difficult to pass anything more than an innocuous civil rights law.

When the Eighty-ninth Congress convened in January 1965, it turned its attention to a few of these procedures and actually stripped the House Rules Committee of some of its powers.[70] But a movement for liberalization of the cloture rule made no headway, and a new joint committee on congressional reform was specifically prohibited from recommending any changes in the rules of either House. Battles for civil rights would continue to be fought in the streets.

How long will Congress continue to make such a negligible

[70] The House adopted a 21-day rule that was far from meaningful than the rule that had been in effect in 1949 and 1950. Now it would be possible for the Speaker to wrest any bill from the Rules Committee as long as he had the support of a majority in the House. This was a major step in the direction of a system of party responsibility, under which the elected leadership of the majority party would not be able to claim that it was helpless to enact the legislative program to which it was pledged.

contribution to the solution of national problems? How long will it tolerate institutional arrangements making it so excruciatingly difficult—except in time of crisis—to pass the simplest ameliorative legislation?

The Promised Land is still far away. There is at this time no agreement even on the direction that reform of the congressional system should take. The most thoroughgoing remedy that has been suggested would involve a realignment of the two major parties, with a new liberal party opposing a grouping of former Democrats from the South and conservative Republicans. Such a solution has much to recommend it. The voter would enjoy a clear-cut choice between alternative policies promoted by disciplined parties, and the party in power could be held responsible for its actions by the electorate. Yet the idea is seldom discussed seriously, for we are told that its adoption would encourage the development of irreconcilable antagonisms which might crack the underlying unity of the American people. The tendency to celebrate rather than examine the institutions of American government is deep-seated. It is not easy to win a hearing for moderate plans to democratize some congressional procedures, let alone for grandiose schemes to recast the two-party system.

There is, however, a strong possibility that in the foreseeable future the conservative bias in Congress will be eliminated and the conservative coalition will entirely disappear. When the subjection of the Negro ends and racial equality ceases to be a scare word, whites in the South will begin increasingly to expect other actions from their congressmen than mere opposition to civil rights. They will want their representatives to be leaders in the fight for social welfare measures—because what region of the nation, after all, needs these measures more desperately than the South? When the bulk of southern legislators start voting for such things as strong labor unions, a high minimum wage, and federal health insurance, it is inevitable that the props under the conservative coalition will collapse, for the Democrat from the South will no longer have any basis for partnership with the Republican from the North.

The precondition of all this is the total emancipation of the

Negro. To this cause, the Civil Rights Act of 1960 contributed little. But the contribution of the Civil Rights Act of 1964 was more significant. And the battle is continuing on other fronts—the voter registration line, the school, the factory, and the street—where filibusters and committee obstruction are out of order. The outcome of these contests may be different. If it is, the legislative process will surely not be immune from the changes that will be wrought.

INDEX

INDEX
Of Congressional Terms